# The Faith Factor

# The Faith Factor

My miraculous journey
of conversion through
faith, failure, and forgiveness.

## Leslie Eddleman

Unless otherwise indicated. All scripture quotations are taken from the The New Catholic Answer Bible, (Wichita KS: Fireside Publishing, 2011).

Published by SonRise Studios, www.SonRise-Studios.com


Acknowledgments:
  Editor: Linda Rohmer Sepanski
  Layout, Design: Michael Hitt - SonRise Studios
  Cover Photography: Images by Nannette
  Photo Credits: Emily Andrews - *Portrait Design* - Jason & Danielle's wedding picture
                 Images by Nannette - 1. Family photo in field
                                       2. Sondra and I


Also, a special thank you to each person who also contributed to the making of this book but were not mentioned.

ISBN 978-1-7326696-0-4 (hardback)
ISBN 978-1-7326696-1-1 (ebook)

Printed in the USA.

*My heartfelt thanks go out to Linda Rohmer Sepanski, for her tireless dedication in pouring over my words in The Faith Factor and helping me make sense of it all. Thank you for your servant's heart and for being one of those "holy women."*

# Contents

# Foreword

My purpose for writing this book is first and foremost to give my children a history of God's providence in my life and how my faith in God opened doors that I would not have been able to open on my own. Some of those doors were doors to opportunity, and some were cell doors that had imprisoned me. I want my children to always remember Whom they can count on in life's difficulties and Whom to thank for life's victories. I want to rouse my children, and whoever else is led to read this book, to love God and to be so convinced of His mercy that they will turn everything over to Him so to reap a priceless reward.

I am nobody. I am weak yet I know I am perfectly made, by Him and for Him, with all my weaknesses. I do not know where I am going or what is up or down, but my faith in God leads me. I am sure of only this; God loves me and is waiting to answer prayer. It is only when I completely surrender to God and ask Him to hoist me upon His shoulders and carry me throughout the day that I am at complete peace like a child.

I want my children to learn to embrace their weaknesses, because it is through weakness that God shows us His mighty power. If we were strong in everything, our human reasoning would tell us there is no need for faith or God at all. God allows weakness at times so that we will have no other recourse but to have *faith*. Weakness, what a wonderful gift!

# Part One

# Spoon-fed

# 1

# The Great Impression

There's a hag in my mirror. She crept in around age forty and she just keeps getting uglier and uglier. She vaguely resembles the woman that used to greet me, but that woman departed years ago. As I stare at the hag in the mirror, I succumb to the realization that youth is fleeting. No truth is more evident than that, especially to a forty-eight-year-old desperately trying to hold on to it.

I'll never forget the words my sweet six-year-old nephew, Strider, said in response to overhearing a conversation I had with his mother, my sister, about the consequences of aging. He so innocently tried to console me as he said, "Aunt Leslie, don't worry, I know you're not old. You just *look* old, but I know you're not old." He made me laugh and I thanked him for his compassionate heart. After all, inner beauty is what really counts. Yeah, right!

I wasn't a very pretty child either. I was a high spirited, bony little girl with brownish-gray tetracycline-stained teeth, a result of numerous doses of antibiotics for ear infections when I was an infant. My hair was a short, shaggy mess, and my nose was full of freckles and constantly clogged from allergies. I knew my sister was prettier than I, but I was quite oblivious to the extent of my homeliness until I was "enlightened" one day while visiting the dentist. Or so I thought.

During my regular checkup at the dental office (I must have been old enough to read, but just barely), I noticed my dental chart read: "Leslie Hess (girl)." I found that very curious, so I looked at my sister's chart to see whether the word "girl" was written on hers as well. No, just mine. I thought I must have been so ugly that the dental staff couldn't tell whether I was a girl or a boy. I was convinced that my mother cut my hair too short and this was the reason for the mix-up.

That same day, my dentist explained to my mother the reason for my bright red, gummy smile: it was the side effect of being a mouth breather. "Of course I breathe through my mouth," I thought. "Who doesn't?" I asked my dentist how he expected me to breathe if I didn't use my mouth. He said, "Use your nose." I was dumbfounded. That was the craziest idea I had ever heard of! I never knew my nose was for breathing. I thought it was just for blowing. On the way home from the dental visit that day, I experimented with using my nose to breathe, and just as I thought, nothing went in or out; except snot.

Alongside all of this, to make things even worse, I was

brutally honest. My mouth wasn't equipped with a governor (a fancy word for a braking system) so I said what I thought and I meant it. Thank goodness my feet were small, because they were often in my mouth. Once I overheard my cousin say, "If you ever want to know if your butt is big just ask Leslie. She'll tell you the truth!"

Being brutally honest with a run-away mouth in the days of political correctness has placed me in numerous awkward situations and lost me many "friends." I have grown familiar with the humiliating taste of crow, as I have been forced to eat it countless times in the company of family, friends, coworkers and acquaintances. Actually, my closest friends seem to appreciate my honesty and have been rubbed wrong so well that they've developed immunity to my honest-truth abuse. I never apologize for the truth, only for the hard feelings it creates. I figure if I notice an elephant in the room, why not say so? Surely everyone else sees it too, right? I'm not good at tiptoeing around the truth, and I never learned to beat around the proverbial bush.

In the early days of desegregation there were still separate water fountains for blacks and whites in Kress' Dime Store. As an honest three-year-old, standing in line at the dime store checkout counter, I taught my mother a hard lesson when I boldly professed, "Look, Mamma, at that fat n-- ----!" The dear woman turned to slap my face, but upon seeing what a small, innocent child I was, she then looked at my mother and knew whom she needed to slap. After all, children are like parrots; they only repeat what they have heard. God was with that lovely woman (and my mother) that day, because she was given the gift of temperance and withheld her castigation.

I had a habit of noticing people and their appearance while in the shopping line. To my mother's chagrin, again, one day at the local meat market, I spied an oilfield worker who had just finished his shift on the rig and was standing in line to buy his bacon. I pointed him out to my mother, and my voice resonated throughout the store as I exclaimed, "Mamma! Look at his DIRTY shirt!" The oilfield roughneck never forgot my words that day, as he reminded me of my honesty every time he saw me in public until I was a young adult. He would belly laugh while asking me, "Are you the little girl who said 'Mamma, look at his diiiiirty shirt'?" He knew I was. He couldn't forget me. I had a knack for leaving quite an impression on the people I encountered. Whether it was good or bad, it was an impression.

*"Who will set a guard over my mouth and upon my lips an effective seal that I may not fail through them, that my tongue may not destroy me."*
*Sirach 22:27*

I grew up in a happy household with my two parents, Frank and Ruth, but everyone called them Frankie and Ruthie. My dad was a very happy man who lavished us with hugs and kisses. We knew we were loved even though "I love you" was never said.

My mother was a good woman who loved us, I'm sure, but she never let those three little words leave her lips. She wasn't big on hugs and kisses, and when I would kiss her and tell her I loved her, she would reply with a frown, "Oh, go on."

I was sixteen years old before I remember Mom telling me she loved me. She had just returned home from a two-day spiritual retreat. When she came into the house I witnessed her hugging my brothers and telling them that she loved them. When she noticed me, she started toward me and I couldn't believe it. "She's not going to tell me she loves me, is she?" I thought. She did just that! She hugged me and told me she loved me. I could hardly believe my ears. I remember going into the bathroom and crying. I didn't realize how much power was in those three little words and how desperately I needed to hear them.

Affection wasn't something mom was comfortable with, but she proved her love for us in her daily duties. She was always home when we came home from school and dinner was on the table every night. She hand sewed most of our clothes, and she came on every field trip our class went on, providing a fried chicken lunch for me that she had cooked specially that morning simply because I requested it.

I have two younger brothers, Gregg and Jason, and an older sister, Sondra. I learned early on that it was not in my best interest to get into a shoving match with my sister. Sondra was sixteen months older than I, a beautiful blonde, smart, athletic, and mean as a pit bull. She could tear your head off in two seconds. I was just the opposite of her. I was an average student, an average athlete, with below average looks, but had an enormous heart.

I knew God loved me, because that was what I was taught in Catholic school, but I longed to be loved by others as well. I was a perpetual "doer" in order to please others. I loved to be praised and complimented for my "goodness."

I was an expert daydreamer, dreaming of good things

and "God" things. I dreamed of high heels, lipstick, evening gowns, long hair, dancing, acting, angels, heaven, Jesus, a handsome husband, and becoming somebody notable. I had a childlike faith that God had something special for me just because...just because I asked Him every day to grant me what I wished for.

---

*"Ask anything of the Father in my name*
*and it will be given."*
*John 16:23*

---

As a young girl, I knew with all my heart that I was the best dancer in the world! No one else knew it, but I did. I took dance lessons at a local dance school, and my instructor noticed that I had a special talent. My mother entered me into various competitions and pageants and I felt at home on the stage. This boosted my confidence even more, and I knew more than anything I wanted to dance on stage somewhere when I grew up.

Even with all my natural dancing abilities and stage presence, I was never selected as dance team "officer" in school, even after multiple auditions. The voting was done by the student body and teachers. I wasn't popular with the students and I drove the teachers nuts with my lack of interest in school work. So even though I was probably one of the better dancers and performers on the dance team, I never advanced into a leadership position. My senior year I auditioned for high school cheerleader, and the only reason I was elected was because the student body rallied against the popular cheerleader. So really, I won my position by default. Throughout those awkward teenage years, God lovingly blessed me with people who encouraged me and He also blessed me with people who discouraged me. Discouragement was more of a catalyst than anything. It kept me moving forward because I was so desperate to prove myself.

I'll never forget Sondra shouting at my mother about which college she should attend. She was extremely bright and was accepted into a very prestigious college in Dallas. My parents were not able to afford that particular college, however, and out of frustration, she screamed, "I should get to go to any college I want because Leslie is too stupid to go to college!"

I knew she was only acting out of frustration, but her sharp one-liner stung a bit and that was just the motivation I needed. I knew then I was going to prove her wrong. I had big dreams and I knew I had talent and creativity inside of me that would bring to fruition all of my desires of being someone illustrious.

I am well trained in the art of positive thinking by my dad. I look at the world through rose-colored glasses and I believe in the power of prayer. I know I won't achieve what I don't first desire because an idea has to be born before it can mature. Dad has always said, "There is so much power in positive thinking."

He is a living testimony to this very concept. The sibling of nine brothers and three sisters, his whole life has been dedicated to hard work. Some of his earliest memories are of getting up in the dark to help milk the cows at the young age of five. He didn't have the luxury of finishing high school and could only read or write at a fifth grade level. While others enjoyed an education, my dad would improve his reading and writing skills by studying the weekly newspaper.

Dad went to work in the oilfield as a roughneck but was not content with remaining there. A positive thinker full of courage and self-esteem, he rebelled against a society that said you can't make anything of yourself without an education. After years of working in the oilfield, Dad seized the opportunity to purchase a gas station. He owned and operated it until he was able to start his own bulldozer service. He did dozer work for many years until eventually he went into partnership with three of his siblings and started an oilfield drilling company. Oil prices were low and money was tight, but he confidently persevered and struggled through the hard times with faith. Dad eventually saw his dreams come to fruition as his business grew and oil prices soared.

My father, who had a limited education, was able to achieve huge success because of his inner drive, confidence, and faith in God. Over a course of twenty years he became a self-made millionaire. But to look at him you wouldn't know it, because he remains humble and genuine. He used to scold me anytime I would judge someone by their appearance or status in society. He told me many times, "Don't write anybody off. Everybody just needs a chance."

My dad is exceptionally inner-driven like his mother, my grandmother. She was the mother of thirteen children and forty-something grandchildren. She was a constant source of love and encouragement for me. She gave me all of the attention I longed for as a child, and she let me know I mattered. A very faithful woman, she nurtured the seeds of my Catholic faith in me.

I will never forget the time Grandmother came outside to play baseball with the grandkids. She had to be nearing sixty years old (but you would have never known it by looking at her) when she stepped up to the plate and sent the baseball sailing into outfield and ran the bases like a gazelle in her dress and high heels, laughing all the while. She knew what was important in life: family, children, and laughter. She never slowed down.

Despite the heavy demands placed upon her, Grandmother always made a point to find time to sit with me and talk about Jesus. She spoke with authority as if she knew Him personally—she did. She taught me the importance of letting people know they are loved. I once read an anonymous quotation in a local newspaper that stated: "Love people so they know how good they are." Most of my life I showered people with love because I wanted them to know how good I was. My Grandmother Caroline lived this simple thought of loving others so they know how good they are. Her life was devoted to service for others. She was completely selfless.

One day, I did something especially praiseworthy and grandmother said to me, "Thank you, Leslie. You are so good. I want to give you a thousand dollars for what you've done." She hadn't a thousand dollars to give to me, but I knew she was trying to impress upon me her deepest gratitude. My reply to her was: "I don't want your money. I only want you to pray for me that I will become as holy as you."

Carefully, Grandmother spoon-fed me my faith and gave me priceless pearls of wisdom throughout my life just by being herself. She encouraged me to remain constant in my Catholic faith. She knew the only way for me to grow in holiness is to truly know who God was, is, and will forever be. Some of my fondest memories are of the times when Grandmother would take me to the nursing home with her. She encouraged me to dance and sing for the residents while she prepared their meals. I enjoyed going from room to room singing and tap-dancing to "You get a line and I'll get a pole..." Now I'm really showing my age! Through her encouragement of me to interact with the residents, Grandmother taught me about the sanctity of life and that all lives have meaning regardless of their state.

We are a culture of do, do, do! "What can you do for me?" is the redundant question of a spoiled society. Instead, it is more appropriate to ask, "What can I do for you." Our Western culture tends to recognize a person's worth by the tangible contribution they can make to society.

Typically, we are a people of waste. We use it, abuse it, and then trash it. Unfortunately, challenged human beings are often viewed as burdensome and irrelevant and subsequently, regarded as persons who are incapable of making a perceptible difference to the "success of society." "Poor quality of life" has become the "diagnosis" for "mercy killings." I want to know who gets to set the standard for "quality of life."

How arrogant a society we have become to think that life and death, and all that is in between, is for our minuscule minds to determine. Only God is the arbiter of life and death and all that is in between.

I've noticed that some of the happiest people I've ever met are those who are mentally challenged, poor, or elderly. Parents and siblings of children with Down syndrome and other developmental disabilities report happy homes and that their lives are filled with joy and contentment because of the very blessings their challenged family members bring to them. It is their very disability that brings forth a tangible impact on those blessed to encounter them.

How can we ever cultivate compassion in our hearts if we are never required to be compassionate? How will we ever truly know God our Creator, Who fashions every single human being, if we don't embrace all life that is generated from Him and for Him?

Life originates from only one source: God, the Author of the Universe. Our God, Who never makes a mistake, has an irreplaceable purpose for every life. Eleanor Roosevelt understood the dignity of the person and the injustice of indifference (at the very least) towards the human soul.

> *Where, after all, do universal human rights begin? In small places, close to home—so close and so small that they cannot be seen on any maps of the world … Such are the places where every man, woman, and child seeks equal justice, equal opportunity, equal dignity without discrimination. Unless these rights have meaning there, they have little meaning anywhere.*
>
> *Eleanor Roosevelt*

I can still remember the faces and personalities of the elderly people I was so blessed to "entertain" at the nursing home. They left an imprint on my heart; an impression upon my soul. I recall pushing them in their wheelchairs and visiting as if we were old friends. I had the privilege of spoon-feeding some of the residents in their beds because they were too feeble to get to the dining room. I knew I was "doing" something significant because I felt so much joy in my heart when I spent time at the nursing home. Through my visits there, I was learning how to serve even though I didn't realize dancing and singing for the residents and feeding the bed-bound was "service." The nursing home was a wonderful training ground for gaining compassion and respect for all human beings, especially the elderly.

On one particular day, while feeding my great-grandmother, Anna, I was explaining to her that I was her great-grandchild on my mother's side. I noticed she was staring intently at my arms. She reached out with her long, bony finger and rubbed it across my arm. I thought she was about to tell me something wonderful, so I listened carefully to her raspy whisper as she said, "You have hair on your arms." I felt duped! There I was, giving her my gift of self and sincere love, and she pointed out my hairy arms! So, I was a hyper, shaggy haired, bony, brown-toothed, gummy smiled little "(girl)" with a clogged up nose, and HAIRY ARMS. Ugh!

As the years went by, my brownish-gray baby teeth exfoliated and new permanent white teeth took their place. Years of painful allergy shots paid off, and I was able to breathe through my nose. My hair grew and I filled out somewhat and I developed into a pretty young girl.

When I turned eighteen I went to work as a dental assistant in my childhood dental office. As I stumbled across my old patient chart, to my surprise I found there were two patient charts with my name. One chart read "(girl)" and the other "(boy)." All of my childhood confusion was made clear. I realized there was another Leslie Hess; a boy! Whew! What a relief. Maybe I wasn't as ugly as I thought.

# 2

# The Trial

When I was nineteen, I took my small-town dreams and dancing talent to the city where I auditioned for the Dallas Cowboys Cheerleaders. Over twelve hundred girls applied for a chance to be a Dallas Cowboys Cheerleader that year, but God was good to me and He promoted me. I joined the squad in 1988.

The gate finally sprang open and the wild horse was running. As a Dallas Cowboys Cheerleader, I was blessed to be chosen among the twelve others from the squad of thirty-two to be part of the elite "show group." The show group traveled throughout the states and abroad and was composed of the strongest dancers on the squad and those who had singing talent. I had definitely been selected on the basis of my dancing and not my singing. Puberty had wrecked my ability to sing on key and voice lessons were to no avail. A perfect stranger had confirmed my lack of singing talent when I was on a personal trip with friends and was invited to sing on stage with the band. A "not so gentleman" in the audience approached me after the show and said with a big, toothy grin, "Darlin, you can dance, but you suuuure can't sing."

The nightly commute from Muenster to Dallas was stressful and the four-hour-practices were grueling. Being part of the show group, I was held responsible for knowing and performing with exact precision anywhere from fifty to sixty dance combinations. The blisters on my feet were agonizing, but the veteran cheerleaders coached us to never burst the blisters, but to instead, bear the pain. This would eventually allow a callous to form over each blister and they wouldn't hurt anymore. I longed for callouses!

I can remember falling into bed at night not knowing the new dance I had just learned and worrying that I would never be able to have it ready for the next night's presentation. There were no excuses for mistakes. I don't know whether God sent angels to me while I slept, but I always woke up remembering the dance that I had forgotten the night before.

That summer was especially trying for me because I was under great duress with the impending death of my mother, who was suffering from breast cancer. I spent my mornings taking care of my brothers and my mother. I remember Mom screaming from the pain of trying to move or roll over in bed. Her body was so filled with cancer that I could smell it. I'll never forget the vile stench of cancer as it eats a person alive. It is a smell that always stays with you. It is something I can't describe.

I remember sitting at Mom's bedside as I fed her last meal to her. As a cool treat for her dry mouth, I gave her a piece of cantaloupe. Even though she had not spoken for days, when I fed her the cantaloupe she looked at me, smiled, and said, "Tastes like... sa sa santaloupe." I just smiled back at her, gave her another piece, and simply said, "It is."

That summer brought a roller coaster of emotions. What I remember the most is the sick feeling in the pit of my stomach caused by my worry, fear, and confusion that God would grant me the enormous achievement of being a Dallas Cowboys Cheerleader only to take away my mother. I had watched her die slowly for a year and a half. She was forty-two. I was nineteen.

It was just before Christmas eighteen months earlier when Mom took Sondra and me shopping for presents. I realized something was wrong when she was willing to buy almost anything we wanted. In a gift shop, I found a beautiful plaque with a pair of ballet shoes on it, along with a prayer asking the Lord to guide my feet in ways so graceful that I would remain in harmony with Him. I reluctantly held it up to my mother knowing she would definitely say "no" to this gift because it was a little expensive and frivolous. I'll never forget the look on her face as she read the prayer. She breathed a long, sad sigh and said, "I guess."

Instantly, I became sick to my stomach. I didn't want the gift anymore. I knew in the deepest part of my being that she was dying, and not only that, somehow, I knew she had breast cancer. I don't know why that was revealed to my heart that evening, but sometimes God gives us divine intuition in order to prepare us for future things.

The day after Christmas that year, while ironing the clothes, Mom asked Sondra and me to come into the kitchen because she had something to tell us. She began to weep and couldn't speak so I spoke for her. I said, "You have breast cancer, don't you?" Still unable to speak, she just nodded, weeping. Then I asked a hard question "Is it in your lymph nodes?" This was the one thing I understood about cancer: you don't want it in your lymph nodes, because that meant death. Again, Mom nodded.

She was devastated and consumed with the fear and worry of leaving behind four children, two of them still in grade school. Over the course of a year and a half, she had tried to distance herself from us as much as she could so that my brothers wouldn't have to witness the decaying process that precedes death. She wanted life to remain as normal for them as possible. She fought a valiant fight, but didn't win.

My mother's death was a turning point in my faith journey. Again, I felt duped. All my prayers were for nothing, I thought. The wrenching in my stomach was unrelenting. I worried so much about my younger brothers who were left without a mother. Mom had raised me and my sister, but the boys were only to enter the sixth and ninth grades that fall. With my older sister distant and busy with college life, I felt incredible pressure to fill the void in their lives. I tried desperately to keep some order in the home. I can remember trying to cook fried chicken for the first time. I had never learned how to cut up a chicken, so I did what I could. It was a poultry mess! None of the pieces were identifiable, but we ate it.

Over the summer of my mother's death, my heart had grown hard and I didn't love as much as I used to. I didn't want any friends, nor did I feel like I needed them. The compassion I used to feel for the less fortunate went away, and I didn't care to hear about other people's heartaches or difficult circumstances. Even though I was growing into an attractive young woman on the outside, on the inside I grew uglier and uglier. There was a beautiful woman living in my mirror but a hag was in my heart. I grew jealous of my cousins who had mothers to spend time with and I was angry that I had never gotten to really know my mother.

At the age of nineteen, I was just coming off those awkward, rebellious teenage years and I was maturing into a young woman. I began seeing my mother through a different pair of eyes. I was learning to appreciate her more and I enjoyed spending time with her. I had just started playing golf about the time she was diagnosed with cancer. This may seem trivial, but I wish I could have played one round of golf with her. I regret that I had never had the opportunity to tee up a golf ball and challenge her to a round of golf.

In my shriveled heart, I felt like I had been dealt a raw deal and that the only reason I had made the Dallas Cowboys Cheerleaders squad was because God was trying to smooth things over. Maybe He was. I would have easily given everything back in order to keep my mother. But God doesn't work that way. He was producing something in me that I did not recognize at the time. It took me many years before I realized that God had cultivated a seed in me that I would need at many different stages of my life. It was the seed of endurance.

Despite my wallowing in a mud pit, God continued to bless me, even though I acted like an insufferable spoiled brat, holding a grudge against Him as though I deserved better.

---

*"But who indeed are you, a human being,*
*to talk back to God?"*
*Romans 9:20*

---

Fortunately, God's love is never conditional. Thank God I didn't receive what I deserved. God didn't change His opinion of me, even though my opinion of Him was sorely lacking. As I licked my wounds, God continued to faithfully and gently nurture me. I didn't lose my faith, it just changed. It sat dormant for a while, but slowly, over time, I was able to accept God's peace that He longed for me to have.

When fall came, it was time for me to go back to college and I would be changing dorm rooms that semester. I had been rooming with a sweet girl on a sorority floor filled with bubbly, spoiled girls who wore lots of hairspray, expensive clothes, and fake smiles. My roommate and the other members of that particular sorority had tried to persuade me to join, but I knew they only pursued me because I was a Dallas Cowboys Cheerleader and that they had no real interest in me, other than the prestige of my title. So, I was to move into another dorm room with a different girl my age.

As I turned the key and opened the door to my new room, I smelled a familiar odor that made my stomach turn. The scent was still vivid in my memory. It was the smell of sickness. My first thought was, "No, Lord. Not again." I didn't know what or whom I was about to encounter.

I encountered Gretchen. Gretchen was God's way of

spoon-feeding me back to life. She was a sickly young girl who spent her weekends at Children's Hospital in Dallas receiving "treatments." She was a beautiful girl inside and out. The steroids she was on made her chest barrel shaped and her face full. Her legs were skinny and sometimes didn't work. She was accustomed to wheelchairs and walkers but was able to walk most of the time.

God placed Gretchen in my path to remind me of the beauty of life. I will never forget how she loved life, all the while never complaining about her disability. I had been given a great gift when I was placed in that dorm room with Gretchen. We were God's blessing to each other. I was the "super star" roommate that she needed to boost her spirit, and she was the super star roommate I needed to bring my spirit back to life. Over time, I was able to feel compassion again. Gretchen and I shared countless pizzas, stories of Children's Hospital, and narratives of the drama taking place with the Dallas Cowboys Cheerleaders. We were good for each other's soul. She kept me grounded, and I kept her soaring.

After her graduation, Gretchen went on to work with hearing impaired children through deaf education. She devoted her life to service for the special needs of children. In her early forties, she finally succumbed to her lifelong illness and went to be with the Lord in heaven. I rejoice knowing that she is not sick and suffering anymore and that she is finally dancing with perfect gracefulness; like a ballerina, without the assistance of a walker or wheelchair.

Aside from the many hours of dance practice, countless high kicks, show presentations, personal appearances, and game day performances, a great reward that came with being a Dallas Cowboys Cheerleader was the commitment to the community carried out through our stewardship of time and talent for those less fortunate. Our weekends were spent visiting nursing homes, orphanages, soup kitchens, drug rehabilitation centers, and hospitals. Once again, I was "serving" others by letting them know they mattered.

I was reminded of my childhood when I went from room to room lifting spirits, as I was now doing as a young woman. We visited many orphanages and met so many children who desperately desired adoption. I remember being heartbroken by the children who, although their basic needs of food, clothing, and shelter were being met, lacked the fundamental need that every child desires—the love of a parent.

On one particular occasion when visiting a drug rehabilitation center, I met a tattooed young man named Jesse. He couldn't have been more than twelve, but he was there "drying out." He told me how all of his family members were "kilt." He gave me a detailed account of the knife killing of his cousin, who was part of a gang. There was no one left for him. "They're all kilt," he said.

Jesse was one of the boys I met again later in the year while on a visit to an orphanage. I couldn't help but think of my brothers at home, who were about his age. God had blessed my family in abundance, and I couldn't even begin to understand the immense evil that submerges innocent lives. I remember being thankful for my home and family, but I never fully understood just how blessed I was. Even now, I'm not sure I truly grasp the enormity of God's favor over me.

I spent time reflecting on how God remained with me,

constantly comforting me, guiding me, and protecting me through my mother's illness and death. I thought about one particular time when I went to visit her in the hospital in Dallas and how He covered me with His divine protection that day.

At the time, I was eighteen and fearless. I didn't think anything of jumping into the car and driving an hour and a half to the city alone. One evening, I made the trip to Saint Paul's Hospital to visit my mother by myself. I parked my car in the parking lot, made my way through various corridors in multiple wings of the hospital, and traveled up elevators, until eventually I came upon my mother's room. I can't remember the visit I had with my mother very well, but it was what came after the visit that I can't forget.

When it was time to leave the hospital, I became more and more confused about which way I was to exit the hospital. It was as if I was in a life-sized game of Labyrinth. The corridors all looked the same. I couldn't remember which entrance I had used or how many times I had taken the elevator. By this time, it was dark outside, and making things even worse, the needle of my inner compass was spinning, and I had lost all sense of direction.

When I finally exited the massive building, I had walked only a few steps before a patrol car came along side me. I was greeted by a friendly security guard, who smiled at me and asked whether I needed help finding my car. Feeling a bit disoriented and nervous about being lost and alone in a big parking lot in the city, I gladly accepted his offer of help and climbed into his car. I remember winding our way through the various parking lots to my car. Curiously, the security guard never asked my name or whom I was visiting. As a matter of fact, I found it very peculiar that he never asked me what I was driving or what my car looked like. It was as if he already knew who I was and exactly where I had parked. The security guard safely delivered me to my car, stopping next to it without any directions from me, just as if he had parked it there himself.

I was very thankful and so relieved to be back in my car heading home. The next morning when I called my mother to see how she was doing, she said, "That man came to my room and told me that he helped you to your car." I knew then that I had been in the company of an angel. There was no way that mysterious security guard could have known whom I was visiting. After all, I never mentioned who I was or my mother's name to him. I am certain the angel was sent to assist me in getting home safely. God reminded me that night that He is with me and He proved that He will always provide the protection of His angels to help me get safely "home."

*"For God commands His angels to guard*
*you in all your ways."*
*Psalm 91:11*

With time, I healed from the emotional bruises that came with the pain of losing my mother. I know there will always be a void in my heart that only my mother can fill and scars from the wounds that come with tragic loss. I also know; however, it is these very battle wounds that help form us into the persons God wants us to be.

If we are meant to endure long-suffering trials only to

recuperate fully with no battle scars and no memory of the pain we experienced, how then are we to spiritually mature? If all the unpleasant memories of watching my mother die were erased, and my heartache was forgotten, that would be a far greater loss than her death. My suffering would have been for nothing. I would never have been able to cultivate the wisdom and understanding that God had planted in me through my suffering, nor could I ever draw from the rich source of perseverance and stamina that God provided me through that long trial.

I know that pain and long-suffering trials are for our good. I know this because of my faith in Who God is. He is a loving Father who wants us to crawl into His arms and let Him Love us eternally. God desires our love so much that He allows periods of grief and pain so that we can draw closer to Him and understand with our limited human perception the depth of His love for us.

No act of violence, pain, or suffering is for naught. God's love for us is so intense, that He will allow anything in our lives in order to get us on our knees. So many times, we only turn to Him when we are in trouble. Like the familiar parental phrase given just before a child is punished, "This is going to hurt me more than it hurts you," God never rejoices in our suffering. He only wants the very best for us. We should never think, however, of our suffering as punishment. Sometimes good and holy people are allowed to suffer in order for others to witness their faithfulness. A simple acquaintance may be the benefactor of our suffering through our faithfulness and steadfastness in accepting God's holy will. In our faithful endurance of hardships, God nurtures His seeds of faith in us by granting us His gifts of fortitude, patience, endurance, and trust.

I know no matter what God has planned for me, I can't change His mind. I have to change my mind. I have to desire His will, His thoughts, and His heart. I know God is loving and all good and He would never do anything to harm me. I know this because of my faith in His character. We have nothing but our faith to get us through this life and to the next.

---

*"Consider it all joy, my brothers, when you encounter various trials, for you know that the testing of your faith produces perseverance."*

*James 1:2-3*

---

# 3

# The Fairytale Husband

As months grew into years, God opened another gate for me. I was accepted into the Dental Hygiene Program at Texas Woman's University. I had spent two years in the dance program, and I had started to wonder whether I could do more than just dance. I distinctly remember the "aha" moment when I decided to pursue a career other than dance. I was eating lunch with my twenty-eight-year-old friend, who was also a dance major, and who had no plans of ever graduating. She loved to wear old and shabby clothing and embraced the "starving artist" lifestyle. As I watched her peel her banana and then her orange, I looked at my club sandwich stacked four decks high and thought to myself, "She likes being poor. She is satisfied with less…" "Not me, I like meat!" The light bulb went off and I realized that my dreams of being a dancer could be, and already were being, fulfilled without a degree in dance. I thought about my short career as a dental assistant the year after high school, and I realized I probably had an edge over the other dental hygiene students who had not had a year of dental assisting experience. I turned in my application to the Dental Hygiene Department and was accepted almost immediately. I entered the program that fall and found another talent that only God knew I had: picking stuff off people's teeth! Oh, what fun! I did well and graduated in 1991 with a degree in dental hygiene and a minor in dance. I was the dancing dental hygienist! Perfect!

All things were falling into place, and soon my prayers for a fairytale husband would be granted. God guided me to the right place at the right time and I met Coy Eddleman, the love of my life. I found him at an old, dirty gym that I had sought out for the sole purpose of meeting my future husband. I knew that not too many women would be members of that particular gym just because of its rough exterior.

As I entered the gym, Coy was the first person I laid eyes upon. He had one foot up on the bench and was leaning over onto his knee talking with his friend. I thought he was the best looking-man I had ever seen. I remember saying to myself, "He's the one." I just had to convince him I was the one.

We soon began dating. Coy says he knew I was the one for him on our first date when he watched me eat a plate of lasagna in about ninety seconds and finish my meal by wiping up the sauce with my bread. He liked that I was genuine and didn't put on airs to impress him. He liked my honest-truth personality and thought it was a refreshing change from some of the other girls he had dated before me.

Coy was good looking and he knew it. After a few months

of dating, Coy, in all his arrogance, said to me, "Honey, don't tell me you love me." After I finished laughing, I replied, "Don't worry, I won't!" He didn't quite know how to handle my response. I guess he was accustomed to women falling at his feet and telling him they loved him. Well he didn't get that from me. He had met his match.

After meeting Coy's mother on a dinner date, she turned to him and said, "She's your Waterloo." Because I didn't pay attention in history class, I didn't know what she meant by that, but then she explained Napoleon's defeat at Waterloo. Aha.

We dated four years before I told Coy I wasn't going to wait forever to get married and that I had made an appointment with the Catholic priest for pre-marriage preparation classes. I told him that if he wanted to marry me, the meeting was Friday night at seven. On our way to the meeting on Friday, Coy proposed. It was official.

We married in the Catholic Church in my home-town. Coy, however, had not yet been baptized and vowed he would never become Catholic or live in Muenster. Going to church as a couple was more of a crusade than a blessing. Some of our fiercest battles were fought right before or just after Holy Mass. I should have noticed the hissing. There was a spiritual war being raged against us as we embarked on our important journey as a young married couple. We were to make monumental decisions about faith, children, careers, and God's will versus our own will.

Unfortunately, I didn't make wise choices in friends at this time of my life and I was easily persuaded against some of the moral teachings of my faith that I had grown up with. I worked for a short time in a busy dental office in the Dallas Fort Worth metropolis where I was surrounded by "good" people with bad habits. I allowed myself to drift from my faith and fall into the sin of "self." Sin became comfortable.

My conscience was dulled and my tendencies toward indulgence mocked God. I cherry picked the rules that were convenient for me to follow as a Catholic, with the obscene arrogance that somehow, I knew better than the two-thousand-year history of the Magisterium of the Church. I took for granted God's forgiving nature, with little effort to be obedient. Because I let sin separate me from God, I was unable to hear His voice within my soul. I remained deaf to God's gentle whispers for a time. I was self-absorbed, self-centered, and self-promoting.

So many sins were born from my selfishness. My ego agreed with society that I was the master of my domain. I held the notion that children were more of a burden than a blessing. I blocked God's purpose for my marriage through the practice of birth control even though my Catholic faith affirms that the practice of contraception is intrinsically evil. I willingly embraced grave sin for the convenience of having my will instead of being open to God's will. I believed the age-old lies the "feminists" were selling, that women have the right to suppress their feminism...what? I traded in my feminism that God had so wonderfully blessed me with for the lie that, somehow, I was more feminine by suppressing the beauty of my feminism. Is your head spinning yet? It sounds ridiculous, doesn't it? That's because the lie is so ridiculous!

———

*"Sometimes a way seems right to man,*
*but the end of it leads to death."*
*Proverbs 16:25*

———

The Catholic Church stands firm in the truth that "contraception is contrary to our sexual nature."[1] It prohibits the very purpose for which God created sexuality. Somehow, our society has come to embrace material things as a replacement for children. Careers, fortunes, and material possessions take precedence over new life. No Catholic, nor any Christian, can dispute the many Scripture passages that promote childbearing and oppose barrenness.

In fact, all Christians opposed birth control until the 1930s. The sin of contraception did not suddenly go through a divine metamorphism at that time and become something pleasing to God. Nor did artificial contraception free itself from the grave sin that is attached to it. No, our *behaviors* changed radically, and the sin of robbing God of the fruit that comes from the sexual union became widely accepted.

Society's attitude toward contraception makes a mockery of God's divine plan of natural law and order of the way the human body was designed to flourish. The act of contraception angers God so greatly that He brought death to Onan because of it.

*"Onan....whenever he had relations with his
brother's widow, wasted his seed on the ground to
avoid contributing offspring.... What he did greatly
offended the Lord, and the Lord took his life."*
*Genesis 38:9-10*

The Catholic faith recognizes God's theology of the body and allows couples to work with the fertile and infertile periods of a woman's cycle to either avoid conception or embrace it through natural means. God knows our human weakness and therefore, He brilliantly designed the woman's body to be fertile for conception only three to five days out of each month. Self-control is required of a married couple if children are not desired during a fertile time of the woman's body if the couple has just cause for avoiding contraception at that particular time. The fact that so many Catholics have large families leads to the misconception that God's science of the body doesn't work. Nothing could be further from the truth. So many Catholics and non-Catholics who embrace this God given science are led to a deeper and more profound respect for life. They come to acquire a logical understanding of God's design for the human body and the divine blessings that children bring to a home.

I knew I wanted children, but in my time, when I was ready. I didn't want to submit to the teachings of the church. I didn't want to have to pay attention to my own body and learn the beauty of its design. It was just too easy to take a "pill." The Catholic Church says we can have children in our time, not through the disobedience of contraception, but rather, through the natural means with which God Himself has gifted us. My sin of practicing contraception was linked to my sinful desire to please myself and live a lifestyle of my choosing instead of submitting in obedience to God's will.

Through contraception I freely chose sin and embraced it boldly. But God, through His great mercy, sent holy people into my life to show me the truth. God changed my heart and I was willing to follow His direction. The hard part was bringing Coy on board with the idea of being open to life. Coy had a hard time accepting the Church's teaching on contraception, and so the feuds began. While arguing the topic with him one evening, I had no more words of wisdom, so I spouted out the only thing I had left, "Who do I need to worry about making mad, YOU or GOD?" His eyes were opened, and over time his heart changed.

———

*"Children too, are a gift from the Lord, the fruit of the womb, a reward. Like arrows in the hand of a warrior are the children born in one's youth. Blessed are they whose quivers are full. They will never be shamed contending with the foes at the gate."*

*Psalm 127:3-5*

———

# 4

# No Room for Gray

No two sins are independent of each other. All sin is connected to the root of selfishness. Selfish desires bring about every sin that has plagued man from the beginning of time. Lucifer's sin of pride was rooted first in his focus on self. He wanted to be greater than God. Adam and Eve's sin of eating from the forbidden tree was first and foremost an act of selfish desire. They, too, wanted to be like God. Not all sins are deadly, but all sin is derived from the same root source. Small "venial sin" is dangerously connected to its big brother, "deadly sin," through its root system: selfishness. How can I say the sin of cursing is somehow connected to the sins of murder or adultery? The answer is simple; all sin grows from one original source. Like the Aspen tree, many trees sprout from one root system. The trees appear to be independent of one another but are deeply connected to one root system. I was under the illusion that I was able to form my own opinion as to what was right or wrong simply by how I felt. I boldly proclaimed to be Catholic, yet did not abide by the rules of the faith.

> *No one is Catholic on his or her own terms: not the pope, not bishops or priests, not religious, not lay people. It is necessary to accept with integrity the body of belief which the Church, Body of Christ, holds to be true. Whether one is a member of the company of believers or a theologian or a teacher of the apostolic faith in it, all of us are bound by the Church's rule of faith.*[2]

If our feelings can justify right or wrong, then our moral code is dreadfully flawed. God gives us free will to choose to do right or wrong, but He never gives us the free will to decide what is right or wrong.

Our choices define who we are and who we will become. Our conscience is the best indicator of our state in life, but unfortunately sin had dulled my conscience. I was so easily tricked and fell right into Satan's snare of believing that God's rules for moral living didn't apply to me. After all, I was a good person. I was a "good" person marching straight into hell with my eyes wide open. I boldly ignored the rules of the Church in many regards. I was certain that because some of the guidelines were inconvenient for me, the rules need not apply to me.

My sin of disobedience grew strong from its selfish root system. How was I ever going to rid myself of the sin of habitual disobedience if I didn't target the root? Like pulling weeds in the garden, if we only pluck the top of the weed, the weed soon returns. We must pull the weed from its root to prevent it from coming back. Once we better understand the driving force behind our sins, we are able to overcome the sin by digging it up by its root.

How many times have I entered the confessional with the regret and embarrassment of having to ask forgiveness for the same habitual sins? I was not able to overcome my tendencies toward sin because I did not recognize the root cause of my offenses. Once I began to understand that my sins were symptoms of a greater sin culminating within me, only then was I able to attack the root.

When my children have a fever, I don't merely treat the fever. I have to know as an experienced parent of five children that a fever is a symptom of something greater. I have to investigate or take them to the physician for a checkup. I have a responsibility to get medical care and the proper medicine for my children when they are sick. This same mentality applies to caring for our souls as well. Just as our physical bodies get sick, so do our souls. When our souls are sick, symptoms begin to appear. Depression, anger, pride, material obsession, and lustful desires are just some of the symptoms of sin.

How do we treat a sick soul? Well, we must first get down on our knees and beg forgiveness for our sins and secondly, we must ask God to show us what needs healing.

The God of the universe is the best physician for the soul and He will heal us every time we ask for it. But we have to ask and then respond to His treatment prescription. If we have a persistent cough we would go to the doctor and get medicine for it. Well, we can't just pour the medicine into the dosing cup and not drink it; we have to digest the medicine in order to be healed. The same is true for taking medicine for our souls. Whatever God prescribes, we must follow through with it in order to be healed. God always has the perfect prescription for each of our problems. We just need to be willing to digest His medicine.

When our eyes are looking inward toward self, we become sick with the disease of selfishness. Our spiritual immunity to temptation is compromised, and through our lowered defenses, Satan is able to attack on all fronts. Through my illness of selfish tendencies, I was led to believe that somehow God would wink his eye at my sins since I was such a "good" person. What does that mean, "good person?" Am I good because I haven't stolen anything or committed murder? Am I good because I am a faithful wife? Big deal! If the guidelines for being good are to just keep to yourself, don't break the law, don't make anyone mad, and keep your disobedience quiet, then it's easy to be "good." Anybody can be "good."

*Sin becomes comfortable when we are convinced of our goodness.*

This mindset prevents obedience to God and separates us from Him, so that eventually we forfeit the salvation Jesus won for us. Not because He takes it from us, but because we freely deny it.

Jesus wasn't kidding when he warned us to diligently seek the narrow path, for few will choose it. Did He mean the narrow path just meant more rewards in heaven for those who followed it, and the wide path of sin still meant heaven, but just not as many rewards? Well, if you're looking at it from the perspective of someone on the wide path, sure that's what it means! Have a nice time in La La Land. But let's get real.

———

*"Enter through the narrow gate; for the gate is wide*
*and the road broad that leads to destruction and*
*those who enter through it are many. How narrow*
*the gate and constricted the road that leads to life.*
*And those who find it are few."*
*Matthew 7:13-14*

———

As my faith develops more fully, I am gaining a keen awareness of the two standards that Saint Ignatius of Loyola understood well: the standards of good and evil. I am firmly rooted in my belief that there is no room for gray in my thinking and virtuous living. In my young adulthood, I drifted from God's graces because of my own free will. I became confused, and obedience was optional while disobedience was accepted. I was content with proudly strolling down the wide path of sin with my nose perched high in the air. I was comfortable with the color of gray.

Gray areas are Satan's cleverly designed plan to confuse us as to what is right or wrong. Gray opens the door to social acceptance of sin. It lures good people into sin with their eyes wide open. When we see the color black we instantly know it is black. When we see the color white we have no doubt it is white. Gray seemingly merges the two together.

If gray were a lukewarm cup of coffee we couldn't bear to swallow it. We would spit it back into the cup, because coffee is supposed to be hot—or iced cold as a Frappuccino, but never lukewarm.

---

*"I know your works; I know that you are neither cold nor hot. I wish you were either cold or hot. So, because you are lukewarm, neither hot nor cold, I will spit you out of my mouth."*
*Rev 3:15-16*

---

With black representing evil and white goodness, the two can never conform to one another. They are immiscible, like oil and water. Thus, the duality between the two standards exists. Gray areas lead us to form our own opinions as to what is good and what is evil. Our opinions do not matter. Truth matters.

Our secular culture insists that truth is relative and whatever a person wishes to believe as true, must indeed be "the truth." No. Truth can never be relative. Relativism is a master lie from the master of all liars, Satan. The Truth, that is Jesus, can never be integrated into the lie of relativism. We have the Truth planted in our hearts through Baptism and the Word of God. The Truth is laid out very clearly for us in the Gospels through the very words of Jesus.

Since Jesus is the Way, the Truth, and the Life how then, can Jesus be relative? He can't be anything but Jesus. He lived in flesh and bones, He died, and He lives in flesh and bones.

————

*"I am the Way, the Truth, and the Life.*
*Whoever follows me will have eternal life."*
John 14:6

————

Our temporal wants and desires are the very things that keep us from this Truth. The Truth is simple. It is not obscure, or gray, or difficult in any way to understand if, in our reasoning, we use the moral code Jesus gave us instead of a distorted rationale that has enveloped society. Cultures, society, secular groups, or religious groups for that matter, cannot choose what is right or wrong.

Society suffers gravely when it holds tightly to the idea that everyone can have it their own way. Yes, indeed we can have it our own way but there are always consequences. We learned in science class about the order of cause and effect, and we have heard the popular phrase "What comes around goes around" many times. Well, this applies to our free will. Just because our sinful choices feel right and good that doesn't mean they won't come back to bite us in the "end."

# 5

# The Big Picture

Coy and I bought our first home in a small, quiet neighborhood at the end of a cul-de-sac in Denton, Texas. At the opposite end of the street there lived an eccentric old man, thin as a rail with stringy, gray hair combed over the top of his balding head. His fingers were bony and his clothes were baggy. He was long and lanky, bent over a bit, and had to be in his eighties in my estimation. I never knew his name but he was a peculiar man who spent his days pushing his lawnmower up and down our street while having a conversation with himself. Some days, I would sit in the yard and watch him move at a snail's pace up the street to my house, then back again. He was always chattering something but never formed sentences or made any sense, until one day when he made perfect sense.

Coy and I were young with new jobs and for the first time in our lives, we had a house payment. We were living out the dreams of married life. At this point, we had not yet embraced stewardship, a way of giving back to God for all the blessings He had given us. It was at this time in my life that God summoned me to a different level of discipleship. This time it was through my pocket book.

One day I received a request from my alma mater, Sacred Heart Catholic School in Muenster, for a monetary donation to help support the school. I thought about the request for a moment and reminisced how much my mother had loved that school. She did everything she could to afford a Catholic education for me and my siblings. She spent countless hours in volunteer work and fundraising for the school, as did many other devoted parents. Tuition was a burden on my parents but my mother was adamant that we received a Catholic education. Dad's dozer business was my family's main source of revenue, and the bills outweighed the income many times.

My mother worked at the dress factory until my younger brother, Gregg, was born. She then stayed home to raise us and keep our house in order. She remained steadfast in her faith and made many sacrifices to come up with the cost of tuition for the Catholic school.

My parents were frugal but they never let us know we were poor. After all, we were rich in God's blessings. Mother knew an education in our faith was the best thing that she, as a parent, could give to us. So, I decided to send a gift of three hundred and fifty dollars to the school as a memorial donation in honor of her.

I placed my donation in the accompanying return

envelope and went straight to the mailbox at the curb. I didn't notice anyone on the street, but as I turned my back to the street and placed the gift in the box and then shut the lid, I was startled by the "old man" who was standing right behind me. He smiled while he pointed his bony finger at me, saying, "You have friends in high places." I didn't know what to say because I was confused as to how he appeared so quickly at my curb. I nervously replied, "I do?" He nodded his head and repeated "Yes, yes, friends in high places." I made my way into the house a bit confused as to why he would say such a thing. First of all, HOW did he say such a thing? I didn't know he could speak plainly or sensibly. Then it hit me…high places! The little old man had just delivered a message to me from "high places." I was thrilled and confident that God was pleased with my generosity, and that my mother was smiling down upon me from heaven. I ran to the window to see whether the old man was still there, and to my surprise he was gone. I went outside to see whether I could spot him down the street; after all, he couldn't have gone far because he was old and slow. There was no sign of him.

I know God uses people to serve as messengers for Him —or maybe the messengers are really angels in disguise as human. Either way, this man was definitely His messenger. This was the first of several visits from the old man down the street. He had an unusual way of knowing just what to say to me and when. The balding, gray haired man will always remain in my memory. I'll never know his name, but I know God had a mission for this little old man. He was to deliver heavenly messages to me.

On Christmas Eve of that same year, the little old man

returned to my driveway to deliver another message to me.

My sister, Sondra, was visiting from Colorado and we were preparing to leave for my dad's house in Muenster for our traditional Christmas Eve gathering. Christmas Eve was my favorite day of the year (other than my birthday), and Coy always seemed to ruin it for me. Or so I thought. He used to make me so mad at Christmas time, because I wanted to celebrate Christmas the way my family traditionally celebrated it, and somehow, he always managed to burst my Christmas bubble.

Really, after looking back, it was my own selfishness that was to blame for my "ruined" Christmas. I acted like a spoiled brat that day, planning our Christmas excursions whether Coy agreed or not. I lost all sight of what Christmas was truly about and I spent the day whining and complaining about Coy to my sister. I became so irate with something Coy had said or done. Maybe it was just his breathing that made me mad; I can't remember, but I recall storming out of the house huffing and puffing insults under my breath. I was determined to leave for Muenster without him.

As my sister and I approached my car, there in my driveway stood the little old man, as if he were waiting for me. He shook his long bony finger as he scolded me, saying, "You need to get the big picture!" I stopped dead in my tracks and stared, speechless. As he turned to go, I climbed into my car and Sondra asked me, "What did that old man say to you?" I replied, "He said I needed to get the big picture." She looked at me and said, "Yes, you do."

It was a long drive to Muenster that evening. I felt like a fool, and deservedly so, because I was a fool. My eyes were habitually turned inward, focusing on myself. How then, could I look straight ahead and see the big picture right in front of me? Most of the misery and disappointments Coy and I experienced were a direct result of my enormous ego. I was a selfish, pigheaded fool who missed the meaning and importance of Christmas because I let myself drift into a fog of selfish, sinful tendencies.

I didn't have a sound understanding of the spiritual state my life was in. I was like so many other "good" people, taking God's mercy and love for granted, and I had stopped cultivating my garden. I had let weeds grow up and choke out my faith to the extent that I couldn't differentiate the weeds from the flowers. It was just like the callouses I got from the go-go boots I wore when I was a cheerleader. The boots rubbed a painful blister every time I wore them, until eventually the blister formed a callous, making the boots comfortable to wear. If we keep repeating the same sins, the sting of the sin eventually goes away when the "callous" forms.

Guilt is a good thing. It is our soul's way of speaking to us to let us know when it is being damaged. We get a stomach ache when we eat too much of the wrong thing. The same is true with our guilt mechanism. It kicks in when our souls are sick…but not if a callous is allowed to form, because then sin becomes comfortable and we no longer feel the sting of guilt.

Satan's clever scheme is to confuse us and fool us into thinking sin is harmless as long as we're "good." Even worse, his aim is to lead us to believe that he doesn't exist. Therefore, sin is relative. No one understands and believes in the power of God more than the devil. He knows who God is and he desperately wants to keep us from Him. Satan hates humanity and will stop at nothing to destroy us.

*"When God, in the beginning, created man, He made him subject to his own free choice. If you choose, you can keep the commandments; it is loyalty to do His will. There are set before you fire and water; to whichever you choose, stretch forth your hand. Before man are life and death, whichever he chooses shall be given him."*

*Sirach 15:14-17*

As Christians, we are constantly being attacked on all levels. This is nothing new, throughout history Christians have been persecuted, crucified, beheaded, and at the very least, ridiculed for embracing morality and virtuous living. We have to know with all certainty who is on the attack, but most importantly, we must know through our faith that the battle has already been won and that eternal life is ours. But there's that little thing called free will again. God never forces us to accept His salvation. So, we can definitely lose it by denying it.

God clearly sets a path before us and shows us the way to heaven is through Jesus. Jesus is the gate. There is no other.

One day a friend of mine was boasting about the clever way her contemporary church had hung a door in the ceiling to represent the gate to heaven. I thought it was sad that no one thought to hang a crucifix on the ceiling to remind their members Who is the gate to heaven and just what He had to endure to enable us to enter through Him.

*"I am the gate. Whoever enters through me will be saved."*

*John 10:9*

If we believe that Jesus is the door to eternal life in heaven, then we must also be sure of His counterpart, Satan. Satan is the trap door to hell. I call him the "trap" door because he is incessantly stalking and pursuing us like prey trying to ensnare us in his trap. If we find it difficult to be obedient to God out of love and reverence for Him, then we can at the very least, remain obedient out of the fear of spending eternity in hell.

When I was young, I refrained from many sins strictly because of my fear of going to hell. Fire, worms, biting, pinching, gnashing of teeth, and perpetual wailing in grief and agony is a real truth that must be grasped. Yet sadly, rarely is it spoken of. Hell is a reality that has been swept under the carpet because we are in the habit of fooling ourselves that no good God would send His children to a place so deplorable.

Jesus came to save us—and He did, but His crucifixion was not a permission slip to live out-of-control sinful lives. We cannot have it both ways. We cannot choose to live like spoiled heathens and expect the rich reward of new life in heaven just because our mouths proclaim "Jesus is my Lord and Savior." How it must sicken God to hear these words from insincere hearts.

---

*"Are you to steal and murder, commit adultery and perjury… go after strange gods that you know not, and yet come to stand before Me in this house which bears My name and say: "We are safe; we can commit all these abominations again"?*
*Jeremiah 7:9-10*

---

Here is God's answer to His question that He presented in the previous Scripture passage.

———

*"And now, says the Lord, because you did not listen,*
*though I spoke to you untiringly; because you*
*did not answer, though I called you*
*I will cast you away from me…"*
Jeremiah 7:13,15

———

I have to decide each day, "Am I going to serve Leslie, or am I going to serve God?" I can't serve both. I must not deceive myself and say, "Yes, I can serve both myself and God," or fool myself into thinking that I can represent Him well and still live my life to my own choosing outside of His perfect will. This sort of arrogance about sinfulness invites God's wrath into our lives. God's wrath is His reaction to our misdirected piety that ultimately serves as a façade for our own self-interest.

I like to take situations and put them into simple terms that I can understand. Without simplifying God, I am going to take a stab at explaining how God must feel when we misrepresent Him.

When I was the dance director and choreographer for the high school dance team, I took pride in my choreography and painstakingly thought out each movement as it complimented the music. When I taught the dance team members a routine, it was customary to go over and over the movements, breaking down each sequence so they would easily remember the combinations and no part of the dance would be sloppy or confusing.

Because I was working as a dental hygienist at the same time, sometimes I would have to miss practice and the school sponsor would have to step in to help perfect the dance. After missing practice the day before, I was eager to see how well the girls perfected the dance that I had taught them. They performed each step to my expectation until the end. "The big finish" was changed to something very simple, boring, and blah simply because they didn't want to practice. "Who changed the ending?!" I shouted. They all started pointing fingers at each other, and ultimately, blamed the school sponsor for changing the ending that I had worked out so beautifully. "You are not choreographers and your sponsor is not a choreographer!" I bellowed. "If you want to get in front of all those people and dance like that it's YOUR choice, but you're on your own! Don't put my name on that piece of work!" There was no way I was going to allow anyone to announce over the loud speaker prior to their performance that Leslie Eddleman was the choreographer.

Even though seventy-five percent of the choreography was my work, twenty-five percent was a lazy misrepresentation of my work. I was completely embarrassed because even though my name was not announced that night, everyone in the audience assumed that the routine was my choreography.

I don't know if God gets embarrassed when we misrepresent Him, but I'm pretty sure He gets angry, because the Scriptures tell us so. There is no way God is going to allow the facade of conformity to His will when our intentions are self-willed. Our pious attitudes towards our sinful desires makes Jesus look bad. There is no way He would choreograph the perversity, unlawfulness, selfishness, greed, and hate that has enveloped the world. I know also, He would never choreograph a boring, simple, "blah" dance filled with indifference, "whatever pleases you", mediocrity, and self-appointed ignorance to the Truth. I can picture Jesus saying, "You have free will so do as you choose, but don't stick my name on that behavior!"

Seventy-five percent of the choices we make can be in line with God's will, but if we slip in our own choreography here and there, He's going to take notice!

If we are not for Him, then we are against Him. If we are against Him, then we must accept the consequence.

———

*"Whoever is not with Me is against Me."*
*Matthew 12:30*

———

Jesus clearly warns us of the fiery hell that awaits those who choose to live separate from Him. Hell is separation from God for eternity. No hope, love, or life is present there; only death and destruction.

God knows our human weakness and accepts our obedience to Him even if it is merely out of the fear of spending eternity in hell. But He doesn't want us to remain stagnant at that level of thinking. It must sadden our Lord immensely when we succumb to obedience to Him strictly out of fear of Him. This was the primary practice of the ancients that lived before the time of Jesus. Sacrifices and rituals were offered to pagan gods out of fear, not out of love.

God wants us to love Him, not just obey Him. Just as

infants are weaned from the bottle, God eventually requires our relationship with Him to mature into a deeper love for Him. As we are weaned from the bottle, so to speak, God gladly spoon feeds us until we are able to chew solid foods. When we confess our sins, and say an Act of Contrition, we say to God that "We are heartily sorry for having offended Him because we dread the loss of heaven and the pains of hell, *but most of all*, because He is all good and deserving of all our love."

Sometimes we are merely infants in our allegiance to God as our loving Father. Understanding the all-knowing and all-loving nature of God is a gift from the Holy Spirit. What is revealed to us in the Word of God is made manifest in our souls through our diligent search for Him. We must never stop seeking Him. He promises that if we seek Him, we will find Him.

*"And I tell you, ask and you will receive; seek and you will find; knock and the door will be opened to you. For everyone who asks, receives; and the one who seeks, finds; and to the one who knocks, the door will be opened."*

*Luke 11:9-10*

# 6

# Beware of the Snake

With maturity came opportunity and growth. Our family was growing and so was our faith. In 1996, after three years of marriage, Coy joined the Catholic faith through baptism and confirmation during the Easter Vigil Mass. Our first son, Cooper, was born two months later.

When Cooper was two years old and our second son, Hudson, was on the way, it was time for Coy and me to make another epic decision that would substantially affect our faith journey. We said goodbye to our home in Denton and built a new house in my hometown of Muenster, Texas. We understood that raising our family in the small, tight-knit community of Muenster would be healthier for our children than raising them in the city.

Muenster was and is a community of faith-filled people who love God and neighbor—for the most part. Small town life tends to keep people honest because everyone knows everyone else's business.

I was blessed with a job opportunity as a dental hygienist for a good friend of mine, Dr. Elaine Schilling, who had just graduated with her dental specialty degree in prosthodontics. Her practice was in Muenster and I no longer had to commute to the city for work. The clientele was drastically different from the patients I had treated in the city. The bulk of my patients weren't night club dancers, or drug dealers in expensive suits, or business men who spent more time out of the country with their girlfriends than home with their wives. My patients were now dairy farmers, oil field workers, factory workers, stay-at-home moms, and people of faith. The conversations at work were refreshing, and Dr. Schilling was a constant source of encouragement and motivation for me to be "better."

Dr. Schilling reminded me of the very thing I had used to believe as a child, that there is no place for mediocrity. I had slumped down so low as to blend in with and share the same ideas of substandard moral living and indifference as the people with whom I was surrounded with before my move back home. Dr. Schilling reminded me of the perfectionist that was hidden within me, because she was, and is, a perfectionist. She expects only the best from her employees and nothing less.

———

*"My brothers, if anyone of you should stray from the truth and someone bring him back, he should know that whoever brings a sinner from the error of his ways will save his soul from death and will cover a multitude of sins.*
*James 5:19-20*

———

Dr. Schilling's work as a dentist is exemplary, but her service and obedience to God as a faithful Catholic woman is even more than exemplary; it is honorable. She pointed out my disobedience to my Catholic faith and helped pull me out of the swamp into which I was sinking.

Aren't we all summoned to throw a rope to those among us who are sinking and pull each other out of the mud pit of sin? Showing someone his or her sins is by no means being judgmental. It is our duty to God and to one another.

One day, I had a spat at work. I was defending marriage, while a coworker was insistent that divorce is preferable to an unhappy home. She accused me of being judgmental toward the persons contemplating divorce. I always wonder why people get so bent out of shape when they think other human beings are judging them. I can't condemn anyone. God is the One and only judge. Actually, human "judgment" may be preferable. I would assume it might be lenient compared to what we actually deserve. If we would focus more about what God thinks of our behavior, instead of what others think, we might behave more appropriately. I, for one, am relying heavily on God's infinite mercy. Thank goodness, we have that promise to fall back on.

---

*"Mercy triumphs over judgment."*
*James 2:13*

---

In my exchange with my coworker, I was arguing that, except in cases of physical abuse, the home never has to be fatally unhappy. Our choices in how we respond to one another make a huge difference in our happiness. Often, our pride is in pursuit of some sort of victory at the cost of our family member's happiness. When we go to college we are thrown into a dorm room with perfect strangers and we can co-exist just fine. Why then is it that in the home we can't get along? Selfish pride!

As Christians, we are not called to be happy; we are called to be holy! Striving to be holy brings forth happiness, because when we look to be holy our perceptions change, our choices change for the better, and our hearts change. No one is too weak to strive for holiness. No one is too weak to put aside self and bring happiness to a home. I speak with authority, because I know full well the damage to a marriage when one person is self-seeking. That person was me.

There was a time when I was a wretched wife to Coy. I didn't care for his needs or show him the respect due him. I was tired most of the time from chasing our three small children all day; therefore, I was quick-tempered, rude, and uninterested in my husband. I had to change. Coy couldn't go on much longer living with a wretch. I was making him miserable, and he finally had to sit me down and give me a "State of the Marriage Union Address."

Some of us remember the days when the whole nation would tune in to hear the President of the United States give his "State of the Union Address" by turning on their televisions to any of the five channels that we had back then. It didn't matter what channel; the address was aired over all of them simultaneously. We listened intently to the President's update on how the country was running. Well, Coy very matter-of-factly let me know the condition of our marriage and his opinion of it.

I tuned in, but didn't like what I heard and was ready

to change the channel. I was humbled and my heart was in my throat from embarrassment. I was at fault; therefore, I had to accept the fact that it was up to me to make amends. Painfully, I listened to him as he told me that he was the unhappiest he had ever been in his life. That was tremendously hard to hear, but I recognized the severity of the situation and I apologized. I asked him what I needed to do to make him happy again. It was the hardest conversation I've ever had with Coy.

Even though I could have retaliated and given Coy a list of my needs, God held my mouth shut that time and I knew I had to let my husband know he mattered. There would be another place and time for me to let Coy know my needs, and this time was not it.

God was with us that night as He opened my eyes and helped me see what was right in front of me. I began to pray for my marriage every day, and our marriage grew stronger and more respectful. I don't let a day go by that I don't ask God for His continued blessings over our marriage.

*"Finally, brothers, rejoice. Mend your ways, encourage one another, agree with one another, live in peace, and the God of love and peace will be with you."*
*2 Corinthians 13:11*

As married couples, we must always remember that divorce is ultimately Satan's goal. With the breakdown of the family comes the breakdown of the nation and of the whole world. We must never forget that the Christian family is constantly under attack and that we must remain diligent in keeping family first. We must do away with selfish desires or habits that do not support a happy and healthy home. It is imperative to the survival of the family that parents take into consideration the immense value of their role as models for their children.

Charles L. Allen explained the role of parents perfectly when he wrote:

> *The parents are the greatest social influence on the life of the child. It is the home where the child first learns to respect the personalities of others, to have regard for the rights of others, to learn obedience to the laws for the welfare of all people. A child's respect for both authority and democracy usually must begin, if it begins at all, in the home. So, upon the parent and child relationship in the home rests almost our entire civilization.[3]*

Distraction is the enemy to the home. Games, cell phones and computers keep our noses down and our eyes focused away from God. We must spend less time being distracted by useless games, social networking, and listening to the lies of the social media. If Satan can keep us distracted, he is able to slither into our homes unnoticed, until one day we find ourselves caught in his coils. My Grandmother Hess, after giving birth to her first son, James, was made well aware of Satan's attack on the family.

With no central heat or air in their home in the 1940s, my grandparents would leave the door to their bedroom open at night to keep it cool. When James was a newborn asleep in his bassinet, Grandmother heard him gasping for air. When she got up to check on him she was horrified at what she saw. There was a huge snake in the bassinet! It had coiled itself around the baby and was trying to crush him. Frantically, she ran to the kitchen to get a knife to cut the snake off James. My grandfather didn't know where to cut without injuring the baby. He was panicked as he grabbed the snake and cut it into bits, freeing their infant son.

My Grandmother, who was very wise and faith filled, saw the snake for what it was: a serpent out to devour her child. She knew the snake represented Satan, who roams the world seeking to devour souls, and the spiritual battle between my grandmother and Satan became fierce. She knew this incident was an indication that Satan would be after her children, so she was unrelenting in her faith. Through fervent prayer, she armored herself and her children with the only thing that makes the serpent flee: The Truth of Jesus.

The serpent is always looking to devour our children. He devours our children slowly through distraction. He devours our families through lies of social acceptance of sin. Through contraception, he devours the egg while in the nest. Through abortion, he devours the mother first, and then he is able to get to the young. It is important to know that through abortion, two innocent lives are taken as prey. First and foremost, it's the mother's life that Satan preys upon with clever deceit and slippery coercion with whispers of *"choice... sss"* rolling off his long tongue.

I once heard a story about a young college student who thought it would be cool to own a python. She loved the snake and assumed it must have loved her too since she fed it, held it, and even let it sleep coiled up next to her pillow. She began to worry about "Snakie" when he stopped eating and changed his sleeping habits. The snake went nearly a month without eating the mice and rats she threw into its cage. She figured the snake must be cold at night because it no longer slept coiled by her pillow. It started sleeping stretched out long against her body. So, the young girl took "Snakie" to the vet. She explained its peculiar behaviors and expressed her worry that the snake might be sick. The vet looked at her and said, "Get rid of the snake. It is measuring you to eat you."

If you choose to sleep with a snake, you might get eaten, literally. Choices made in haste often lead to regret, but methodically weighing out the end product of our choices ensures a wise decision. If we considered all things from our deathbed, how different then would our choices be?

Once we get our bearings, we are able to see a python for what it is: a python. We recognize sin for what it is: sin. The python will never be anything less than a python no matter how much we cuddle it and love it. Sin will never be anything less than sin, even though we cuddle it and love it.

———

*"In whatever you do, remember your last days,*
*and you will never sin."*
*Sirach 7:36*

———

How many decisions will we have to live to regret? Well, thankfully, none of them. Unless you've been eaten by the snake, literally! Because of the Truth that is Jesus, we don't need to live in regret of the past. We should learn from the past, yes, but regret it? No. God is outside of time. He knows all things that happened yesterday, today, and that will happen. When we are truly remorseful for our sins and ask God for forgiveness, He forgives us and removes all record of our poor decisions from His memory as a gift to us.

Satan knows our forgiveness, our worthiness, and God's immense love for us. His game plan is to wear us down by relentlessly taunting us with lies so that we might become so despondent and discouraged that we give up. Never give up! The stakes are too high. No matter the sin, no matter the life choices, we are promised forgiveness.

Sometimes we just need to "clean house" to get rid of the junk that separates us from God's goodness. The junk that piles up in front of us and blocks our view of Jesus can be material things that crowd our closets, or sinful habits that are tied to lust, or maybe the junk is human influences. An occasional reassessment of the direction in which our life is going is sometimes needed. If we want to know the direction our lives are heading, we need to begin by taking inventory of our friends and those who influence us the most.

Bad influences in our lives are like a piece of rotten fruit; they draw gnats. We shouldn't want to be a gnat swarming around rotten fruit and we certainly don't want to be the rotten fruit drawing in the gnats. If you are associating with the wrong sort of people, determine first whether you are the gnat or the rotten fruit. Either way, there is impending peril, for the fruit gets thrown out and the gnat gets swatted.

———

*"Either declare the tree good and its fruit is good, or*
*declare the tree rotten and its fruit is rotten, for a*
*tree is known by its fruit."*
*Matthew 12:33*

———

God puts the right people in our path to help direct us. We need only ask Him to show us the way. Imagine God pulling back the veil, enabling you to see your friends cruising down life's highway. Envision which road they are on, the road to heaven or hell. Then picture yourself riding shotgun.

---

*"Limit the time you spend among fools, but frequent the company of thoughtful men."*
*Sirach 27:12*

*Instead, associate with a religious man who you are sure keeps the commandments; who is like-minded like yourself and will feel for you if you fall."*
*Sirach 37:12*

---

# 7

# Holy Women

I know that our move to Muenster was God's way of culling out the negative influences in my life and replacing them with positive ones. God had great blessings in store for Coy and me, but He first had to send reinforcements to rescue me from myself and open the eyes of my heart in order for me to receive them. Those reinforcements came in the way of a group of holy women who lived their faith and proudly professed it. They were humble women who had treasures of godly advice and encouragement for me.

My aunt Mary was one of those holy women. She scooped me up as soon as we settled in. She was glad to have me back home in Muenster and quickly invited me to join her women's prayer group. I went reluctantly, but was moved by the sincerity of the prayers of those holy women. I knew

I didn't want to be as holy as them because they were a little strange (I thought) and I figured I would just strive for "sort of holy" but still "cool."

Ugh! What a rookie Christian I was to think that way. My mindset was still one of self-preoccupation and worry about how others perceived me instead of how God perceived me. I struggle with being holy and sounding crazy, because if people think I'm crazy, then it invalidates what I say…right? Wrong. The words that we speak as witnesses to Christ are always valid because God is pleased by them. We are all called to be holy, but being "cool" and holy is an added perk!

———

*"I tell you, everyone who acknowledges Me before others The Son of Man will acknowledge before the angels of God. But whoever denies Me before others will be denied before the angels of God."*

*Luke 12: 8-9*

———

I continued to go to the weekly prayer meetings and participated in a Catholic women's book study as well. The book study didn't interest me because I wasn't much into reading. So, I generally just faked my way through the meetings and tried to interject at a benign level.

At the time of the study, the demands of working full time and being a mother of two young boys with my third son, Tanner, on the way, I began to feel the pressures of my first vocation as wife and mother and knew my place was in the home, rather than at work at the dental office.

Dr. Schilling's practice was beginning to flourish, and she needed a full time hygienist. I distressed over the decision whether to remain loyal to my employer or to my family even though my gut instinct told me that my family came first. So, I mimicked the pattern of prayer that I had learned from the "holy women" and asked God for an answer to my dilemma. At the end of my prayer for direction, I specifically requested that God make His answer known to me in "black and white" so as to keep me from any confusion. In reality, I was "passing the buck" to God. I wanted confirmation from Him that my cravings to stay home were the right choice. After all, how could Dr. Schilling disagree with my decision if I told her "God said so?"

After a week of anticipating God's answer to my request, I grew restless and began to feel a bit discouraged that God had not yet put His answer on my heart. I resigned myself to the idea that maybe the answer was at my prayer group meeting and surely those "holy women" were going to give me the insight I needed.

Just as I was about to leave for the meeting, I said under my breath, "Lord, you haven't answered me yet. You know I need your answer in black and white. Please, don't leave me guessing." Just then, I remembered the book study and grudgingly retrieved the book that I had not yet read and quickly thumbed through the chapter we were to discuss. As I glanced randomly at the text, I read; "God's wish for you is to stay home with your children and take care of your spouse for a greater reward in Heaven."[4] There it was; God's answer in black and white! I was so thrilled that God saw fit to hear my plea and answer me with such clarity. I shut the book, because that was all I needed to read, and I headed for my weekly meeting teeming with excitement. I couldn't wait to tell the women how God used the chapter in our weekly study to answer my prayers.

As I dramatically recounted my story to them and how God's response was in the very words of the chapter we were studying, I noticed their looks of bewilderment. They seemed puzzled by the fantastic story I told, and I was confused as to why they weren't as excited as I was. Finally, my aunt Mary spoke up and asked, "What chapter did you read?" I told them what chapter I had read, and they all began to smile and discuss among themselves God's goodness. Aunt Mary so lovingly explained, "We're not on that chapter, we're still studying chapter two!"

I'm not sure that phrase can be found again in that wonderful book, as a matter of fact, when I tried to retrieve it for the "holy women", it eluded me. I have yet to go back to that book and try to find it. I just know this: it was there when I needed it.

This was a huge leap in my faith journey. In the months and years to follow, God continued to train me to ask and receive. He opened my eyes to how readily His blessings flow upon me when I rely on His Divine Mercy which He so eagerly awaits to give to me.

This truth of God's Divine Mercy was made evident to me during this particular time of my life as my younger brother, Gregg, was suffering violently from diabetes. His blood sugar levels were so out of control that his numbers skyrocketed off the charts. We suspect he must have suffered from diabetes for months and possibly years before he was properly diagnosed. We worried that his organs must have taken a toll from the abuse of the disease.

Multiple attempts were made to control Gregg's diabetes. Medications however, couldn't curb the erratic spikes and plunges in his glucose levels. Gregg would find himself in the hospital emergency room with his glucose levels soaring to nearly five hundred. The medical staff offered little or no help while his doctors stood scratching their heads, unable to find the right remedy. Gregg was losing hope. He was panicked and fearful. As his older sister, my "motherly" instincts kicked in, but I had nothing to offer him except my fervent pleas for God's mercy on his behalf.

The Feast of Divine Mercy was nearing, and I listened to our priest explain how Our Lord had urged Saint Faustina to encourage others to recite the Chaplet of Mercy as a novena the nine days before the Feast of Mercy. Our Lord revealed to her that He sought to grant unimaginable graces to those souls who would trust in His mercy. God promised to Saint Faustina, that through the chaplet, faithful souls will obtain everything if compatible with His will.

I believed this promise with all my heart. I knew this wasn't just some superstition, because with GOD, through FAITH, we can accomplish all things. I knew it wasn't the recitation of prayers over and over again that was going to magically grant me my wish like a genie in a bottle. No, it is through the repetitious recitation of prayer that our hearts and minds are strengthened as we meditate on our connection with God, The Almighty.

For nine days, I offered my pleas for Gregg's healing to our Lord and trusted in His Divine Mercy. All prayer, when presented with a trusting and faithful heart, is heard and answered. Although, the answer may not always be what we hope for, in Gregg's case, I received more than what I had hoped for.

Directly after my appeal for Gregg's healing on Divine

Mercy Sunday, Gregg's numbers started to stabilize. He went from being an out-of-control diabetic, running the risk of major organ damage, loss of eyes sight, and/or loss of limbs, to the picture of health. He still had diabetes, but his doctors were stupefied at his miraculous transformation. They took detailed records and monitored him closely for over a year.

Other physicians were brought in to study Gregg's case because never before had they seen such a phenomenon of his unexplained change for the better. They questioned Gregg at great length as they tried to find the link to what had turned his out-of-control state of health to picture perfect.

The link was faith. We are all blessed with miraculous answer to prayer that can be easily written off as coincidental, but for persons of faith, nothing is coincidental.

The answer to our prayers for Gregg came in 1998. He is still the picture of health. He does have to manage his diabetes, but he hasn't had any complications from it. Those tortuous days are over. God has great plans for Gregg, and I am certain his trial was a test of endurance and trust.

God draws us to Him through so many routes and avenues. Everywhere we turn, He is setting the stage for us to encounter Him. Sometimes we have to get desperate first; whatever the reason, He wants us to call out to Him.

---

*"Prepare yourself for trials. Be sincere of heart and steadfast, undisturbed in adversity. Cling to Him, forsake Him not; thus will your future be great. Accept whatever befalls you, in crushing misfortune be patient. Trust God and He will help you...."*
*Sirach 2:1-4, 6*

---

# 8

# Grandma Ruthie

Being home in Muenster was good for me, but it brought about feelings of melancholy, because I was surrounded by familiar people and faces that reminded me of my mother. My patients compared me to my mother and often told me how much I reminded them of her by saying, "You sound just like your mother" or "You get your competitiveness from your mother" or "You play golf just like your mother" or "Your mother was funny, just like you." Each time I felt like they were describing a stranger to me, I never saw any of those attributes in my mother. I only saw "mom."

I wished she were here with me so that she could enjoy her grandchildren and tell me how proud she is of me. Little did I know at the time, she *was* with me, constantly watching over me.

It was June 7, the anniversary of my mother's death, and I was running errands with my three-year-old, Cooper. That day I was granted an incredible gift when Cooper told me the most amazing story I had ever heard.

Just as I was pulling into the post office parking lot, Cooper said with excitement, "Mom, I just saw an angel! I saw an angel in my mind!" Knowing that he was learning about God and angels in pre-school, I figured he had a good idea of what an angel might look like—white dress, wings—you get the picture. I half-heartedly replied, "You did? What did the angel look like?" He paused for a few seconds and with a peculiar stare he said, "She looked like your mommy." He immediately had my attention and I said to him, "She did? What did she say?" I expected him to tell me something a three-year-old would envision an angel saying, perhaps, "I'm in heaven with Jesus." But what Cooper said next confirmed that he did indeed see his grandmother, my mother. He smiled a huge smile and said, "Mom, she said she loves you, and she loves me too." He was so excited about the fact that she loved him too that he repeated it at the top of his lungs, "MOM! She said she loves you, and she loves me too, Mom!"

I tried to absorb what my brilliant son had just said to me as I went into the post office to retrieve the mail. When I got back into the car, I glanced at the clock and noticed that not only was it the anniversary of my mother's death, but it was the exact time of her death as well.

God was so good to me. He allowed my mother to visit my innocent son, Cooper, in order for him to console my heart. I knew that my mother was a saint in heaven because of what we had learned in Catholic school. All souls in heaven are part of God's Communion of Saints, while angels are divine beings created by God to serve Him as protectors and messengers. I can only imagine how radiant my mother must have appeared for Cooper to think she was an angel.

I couldn't wait to tell the story to my brothers and sister. I even laughed a bit as I jokingly said to my sister, "I guess I'm just special, Sondra. Sorry you didn't get the same message." Sondra smiled at me with tears in her eyes and lovingly replied, "It's because she knew you needed it the most." I knew she was right. Sondra reminded me that even as a child, I had longed to be loved and needed reassurance more than of any of my siblings.

This wasn't the first-time Cooper had a visit from his maternal grandmother, "Grandma Ruthie." A year before this experience, I was getting my exercise roller-blading through town while pushing Cooper in his stroller. Skating by the cemetery where my mother was buried, I had a strong inclination to take him into the cemetery to place flowers on her grave. Since I had no flowers with me, however, I roller-bladed on by and quickly dismissed the thought. After all, he would be too young to understand the concept of a cemetery, I thought.

Soon, I rounded the corner and arrived at my parked car. I shucked the roller blades and loaded Cooper into his car seat. As I was pulling out of the parking lot, Cooper had questioned me, "Where's Gramma 'Rufie'?" I was a bit confused and asked him to repeat what he had said. He replied adamantly, "Gramma 'Rufie'!" "Where did she go?" He asked as if he had just seen her and was wondering where she went. I tried to pacify him with a simple answer, "She's in heaven with Jesus." He looked perplexed for a moment and then seemed to accept the answer with a soft reply, "Oh."

When I got home I relayed the story to Coy. He argued that I must have misunderstood Cooper since he had never met my mother, and as a matter of fact, we had not yet explained to him that he had a grandmother Ruthie in heaven. As we were debating the situation, unbeknownst to us, Cooper had climbed to the middle shelf of the closet that holds all our photographs. Pulling down a large picture book, he quickly spied a picture of my mother, and said, "Here she is, Gramma 'Rufie'!"

After several seconds, Coy and I picked our jaws up off the floor. Cooper was so proud to be able to show me Grandma "Rufie." I knew then that he must have seen her many times before. I am certain she was and is always watching over us, praying that we make it to our final destination to join her in the company of the saints in heaven.

# 9

# The Brown Paper Bag

As I was nearing my mother's age when she was first diagnosed with cancer, I started to dwell on the fact that I, too, would soon be facing her lot. I had concluded years earlier that I was indeed going to get breast cancer, and I vowed that when I turned forty, I would trump God's plan for me and get a double mastectomy to prevent Him from "giving" me breast cancer.

My mind slowly grew sick with desperation and worry. Over a course of several months, my ten-year anxiety about dying early became so destructive that it brought me to the point that my first thought in the morning before getting out of bed was of death. The familiar wrenching in my stomach that I had experienced so many times when mother was ill greeted me each morning before I even opened my eyes. I was reluctant to leave my children for long periods of time. I rationalized staying home because I thought I was going to die soon and, therefore, I needed to spend as much time with them as possible.

I wanted my children to remember me as a loving mother and so, I mentally tortured myself every time I lost my patience with them. Every decision I made concerning my children was centered on my "impending death."

Satan had a foothold on me. I knew I could no longer live that way and remain out of a mental sanitarium, so I devised a plan. Before I opened my eyes in the morning, I envisioned myself stuffing all of my fears and worries about breast cancer and death into a brown paper bag. I would then hand it to Jesus. Jesus took the brown paper bag from me every morning and unfortunately, I took it back almost immediately. I wanted so desperately for Him to keep it, but my human weakness made it hard for me to trust.

I repeated the process of placing all of my worries into that crumpled paper bag and handed it to Jesus every morning for nearly a month. Over time, I was able to leave it in His hands and resisted taking it back. Each morning the brown paper bag got smaller, until eventually my persistence was rewarded.

One evening as I prepared to take a shower, I raised my arm to perform my usual nightly breast exam. Before I could start the exam, I was engulfed in a profound peace that filled every pore of my body, and every corner of my mind, as it reached to the depths of my soul. The peace was warm and inviting, comforting and soothing. I felt as though I were standing under the warm water of the shower that I had not yet slipped into. God's words consumed me as He said, *"Leslie, your mother's fate is not yours. I have great plans for you…"*

*"For I know well the plans I have in mind for you,"*
*declares the Lord, "Plans for your welfare, not for*
*woe! Plans to give you a future full of hope. When*
*you call Me, when you go to pray to Me, I will listen*
*to you. When you look for Me, you will find Me. Yes,*
*when you seek Me with all your heart you will find*
*Me with you, says the Lord, and*
*I will change your lot."*
*Jeremiah 29:11-14*

He was so loving and reassuring that I was instantly released from the bondage of my fear of death. I put my arm down and I have not thought about breast cancer or death since that glorious moment. Through God's grace and great mercy, I was given a great gift that night; a gift that keeps giving each day. I wake up in peace knowing that my mother's fate is not mine.

I had within my capacity the ability to undo the knot that I was entangled in all the while, but I couldn't attain that freedom until I drew upon the One source that could free me: Jesus. It was only by God's mercy and grace that I was freed. In a cell, I couldn't escape at first, even though God had the door wide open all the while.

The voices in my head were choking out God's gentle whisper for so long that desperation finally took over. It was during this most desperate state that I was able to choose the right weapon to defeat my destroying obsession. It was then that God tenderly picked me up and carried me out of the prison cell. The answer was within my reach all along. Like a sword on my hip, I just needed to draw it out of its sheath.

Saint Ignatius of Loyola was a brilliant man who not only discerned the two standards of good and evil, but understood with great clarity the three powers of the soul. The voices in our head belong to each of the three powers: God, Satan, and our own free will to think what we want. Ignatius found it imperative for the human mind to understand these three powers of the soul. In order to make sound decisions, we must first understand who is doing the talking in our head. Even though it may seem as if we have a dozen voices leading us in different directions, in reality there are only three, each belonging to one of the powers.

Saint Ignatius gives us remarkable advice as to how we are to discern who is speaking to us. He reminds us that when we are able to hear God's voice deep within our souls, we are brought to feelings of comfort and consolation.

The opposite is true for the voice of Satan. His guidance always brings us to despair and desolation. Here is where it gets really tricky though, Satan's cunning tactics can sometimes bring about a false sense of consolation. Eventually, that "consolation" is replaced by despair and distrust, because it is not in Satan's nature to console.

It is important to note that our free will to think the things that we want to think can also lead us to despair, consolation, or false consolation. Discerning the voices in our heads is a complex mind game. We have to study our thoughts, study Who God is to understand His love for us, and know for certain whom Satan is and his diabolical hate for us. Once we have an understanding of the basics: good, evil, and free will, then we can understand the voices in our heads better.

I anguished over the lies that Satan told me for so many

years. I became an expert in mimicking his lies and eventually, I joined in the battle against myself with my own free will and I agreed with his lies. I did not discern that it was Satan's voice in my head. Maybe it was my own free will to "think" myself into devastation. Maybe it was both. All I know is this: I had no other alternative than to seek consolation through Christ.

I was an infant in my understanding of the voices in my head. I was so turned around and upside down that I actually thought I could somehow decide my own fate outside of God's will and still be in line with His will. I was actually afraid of God's will as though it were something harmful. No, God's will for our lives is only to draw us to Him. He wants us close to Him. There is peace and serenity in trusting God's will to the point of willingly accepting whatever befalls us because we know God is love and he only wants the best for us.

Sometime later, Satan tried his best to lure me back into that dark cell, out of which God carried me so victoriously. But this time, I had my head on straight. I applied my knowledge and understanding of God's character with absolute trust and I was able to avoid the snare set for me.

At a regular visit to my doctor, I was advised to do some testing to see whether I had the gene that mutates into an aggressive form of breast cancer. My doctor was adamant and pressed the issue of the testing. She reassured me the testing would be covered by my insurance company since I had a strong family history of breast cancer. She even said, "I would advise the testing because you have small children at home"— reintroducing the same idea that had a stronghold on me so long ago. I asked my doctor what the plan of action would be if the test came back positive. She replied, "We would then discuss surgery."

This was the plan that I had devised so many years ago: a double mastectomy of perfectly healthy breasts in order to intercept God's plans for me. I told her that I was not worried about my cancer risk as much as I was concerned about my cholesterol and vitamin D3 levels. So, I agreed to a blood test to check for those levels. She remained obstinate that we draw an extra vile of blood for the purpose of running the test to determine whether I carried the gene that was responsible for aggressive breast cancer. Because I wanted to avoid confrontation, I relented and agreed to the test.

When I got to my car, I spoke to Jesus about the visit to the doctor. I told Him that I knew no matter what the blood test revealed, I was not destined for breast cancer, because He had told me so. I completely trusted God's word spoken the night He released me from my bondage. I asked God to put a stop to the test and not let it go through if the testing was against His will. This time I didn't need a brown paper bag. I simply released everything into His care.

A few days after my blood test I received a call from the lab. The nurse who spoke to me was bewildered by the fact that the insurance company denied my eligibility for the testing. She strongly encouraged me to allow her to proceed with the testing and explained that the out-of-pocket cost to me would be three hundred and fifty dollars. I politely declined. Again, God took care of me. I asked Him to intervene if the test was not His will, and He did.

*"Trust in the Lord with all your heart. On your own intelligence rely not."*
*Proverbs 3:5*

Our human minds, as intelligent as they are, can't even begin to fathom God's mind. We cannot lean on our own understanding, but must have faith that God is on the throne! Without faith, there is no hope. Without hope, there is no future. Where there is no future, we have only despair. With despair comes desolation through separation from the One who created us. We are meant to be connected to our Creator. It is our faith that is the glue that holds us to God our Creator through His Son, Jesus. Faith is a gift given to us by God and it is up to us to accept it. Our choices have consequences. When we choose to accept Christ, we choose His plan of goodness for our lives whatever His plan may be. Choosing faith in Jesus opens the door to His many blessings and favors that He is eagerly waiting to give us.

This very faith in God is the key that unlocks all the cell doors. Faith conquers all of our fears, worries, and anxieties. It is our faith that affirms that Jesus accomplished all things for our good by His suffering and dying on the cross and through His resurrection. What more could He do to prove His love for us?

We have an eternal reward waiting for us in heaven just because God loves us. All we need to do to obtain it is to be baptized in Jesus, believe in His goodness, and accept His infinite love for us. If we could only begin to understand with our humanness how much God truly loves us, we would be able to trust Him completely with every ounce of our being.

# 10

# Saint Michael:
# "The Sword Bearer"

*Saint Michael, the Archangel, defend us in battle.
Be our protection against the wickedness and snares
of the devil. May God rebuke him, we humbly
pray, and do thou, O Prince of the heavenly host,
by the power of GOD, cast into hell Satan, and all
the evil spirits, who prowl about the world seeking
the ruin of souls. Amen.*

March brought the birth of my third son, Tanner. I
enjoyed my part-time dental hygiene job and the
luxury of staying home with my young children. My oldest
son, Cooper, was attending the Catholic preschool that I

longed for him to attend. He was learning his faith at school and I did my part at home as well to nurture him, and all my children, into a loving relationship with Jesus.

At night, I told them stories of Saint Michael the Archangel. Being boys, they loved stories about swords and fighting, and they knew Saint Michael was the "tough guy" who, by the command of God, battled Lucifer and threw him out of heaven.

One night, about fifteen seconds after we had completed our prayer for the protection of Saint Michael, the toy sword in the chest sounded off. It made the distinct sound of a sword being drawn from its sheath. The boys were astonished by this and began questioning me whether that was actually Saint Michael drawing his sword.

Cooper knew it was the battery-operated sword randomly "going off" in the toy box, but he was still fascinated by how it had sounded off just after our prayers to the "sword bearer," Saint Michael. I explained to them how God allows things like that to happen to reassure us that our prayers are being heard, and yes, indeed, it was a message to us that Saint Michael was near.

Three times in the course of several months this same thing happened. After praying our nightly prayers for protection, the sword would sound off. Never again during the day would we hear the sword; only after reciting the Saint Michael prayer would it ever "sing."

The beauty of the story is this: Cooper had decided that we needed to change the batteries in the sword, so when I went to replace the old batteries with new ones, I was delighted by God's cleverness; there were no batteries in the sword!

Saint Michael remains with our family as our special protector, and I thank God for the intercession of Saint Michael. Many times, I have called upon Saint Michael for protection, but never was it more imperative than the time I once again found myself alone in a parking lot.

It was late winter and I was seven months pregnant with my fourth child, Ruth Ann. Tanner was about to turn four that spring, and he was my constant companion during the day while the older boys were at school. Tanner and I went on a trip to the outlet mall to purchase some maternity wear. We arrived early in the morning and the parking lot looked like a ghost town. The place was desolate except for an eighteen-wheeler parked near the far end of the parking lot. I parked my van fifty yards or so from the store entrance, and Tanner and I proceeded to the store and made our purchases.

As I exited the store, I immediately sensed that we were in danger. I paused for a moment to look around, and even said to myself, "What am I in danger of?" I noticed two teenagers at the opposite end of the outlet mall walking away from me, and I knew there was no need to be leery of them. Just then, I heard internally a voice say to me, "You're in danger. Pick up Tanner and run!" Before I could think, I began reciting the Saint Michael prayer for protection while I scooped up my four-year-old and ran as best a seven months pregnant woman could run.

I made it to my van and put Tanner in his car seat, buckled him in, jumped into my seat, and hit the door lock switch as quickly as I could. The moment I locked the doors, a large man appeared at the rear passenger side of my van. I am unsure whether he had been crouched down hiding behind my van waiting for me or we just had a foot race. All I know is this: I saw him against my van the moment I had locked my doors and was safely inside.

He must have heard the doors lock, as he quickly pulled the collar of his coat around his face and swiftly walked away. As I watched him, I tried to make sense of what had just happened; or what hadn't happened. One thing was for certain: Tanner and I had been intended to be the victims of something sinister, but God had intervened.

As I examined the parking lot, I noticed my van was the only vehicle except for the lonely truck parked suspiciously at the end of the lot. I assumed the man I had seen was its driver. I knew with all my being he had evil intentions for Tanner and me. For weeks, I pondered the events and still to this day cannot fathom how I was able to get safely inside my car without his intrusion. Was an angel holding the door shut so he could not enter my vehicle, or did I, a seven-months-pregnant woman carrying a four-year-old, outrun this strong, muscular man? How did I escape the danger of which I had been forewarned?

Only by God's grace was I able to escape the harm that was intended for Tanner and me. God always equips us with what we need, including our senses, and especially, that inner voice that we call "instinct."

I cannot deny that God placed His angels around us that day and countless other times that He has made their presence known to me. I know I have a guardian angel that has charge over me, but it is in times like these that the unseen is made very apparent. I realize that God spared us from harm that day because he has a greater plan and a purpose exclusively for Tanner and me to fulfill in this lifetime.

---

*"No evil shall befall you, no affliction come near*
*your tent. For God commands the angels to guard*
*you in all your ways. With their hands they shall*
*support you lest you strike your foot against a stone."*
Psalm 91:10-12

---

When I was young, my grandmother, Caroline, insisted that her grandchildren wear a blessed scapular around their neck. She told us it would serve as protection from harm and evil if worn in faith. Many good Christians wear a religious emblem of some sort around their neck as a reminder of their faith and to serve as an outward expression of that faith. Usually it is a cross or blessed medal. A scapular is similar in that it is a sacramental of the Catholic Church, and it serves as a reminder of our devotion to our Lord through the intercession of His Blessed Mother.

"The Brown Scapular" was revealed to Saint Simon Stock by Blessed Virgin, Mary, herself. It was divulged to Saint Simon that anyone who wears the scapular faithfully as an expression of devotion to the Blessed Mother would be granted the grace of final perseverance until their death.

The scapular is to be worn by the faithful around the "scapulae," or shoulders, as a suit of armor. Our Blessed Mother, delighted in caring for her children, points us to Jesus while she places her motherly protection around us. She always remains behind us so that we can keep our eyes fixed on Jesus, who is before us.

Grandmother insisted that when we wore our scapular we were putting on Mary's intercessory protection. She warned us that we should never view the holy scapular as a good luck charm, but to wear it as an act of faith in God, who lovingly grants Mary, the mother of His beloved Son, Jesus, guardianship over His children.

No one is more convinced of gaining our Blessed Mother's intercession through the brown scapular than my cousin, John, and his family. John's six-year-old son, John Louis, was in a horrific accident as he was run over by a 16,500-pound tractor, twice. One afternoon, as John was plowing the field, he accidentally backed over little John Louis, and then ran over him a second time as he took the tractor out of reverse and drove forward. Even after being crushed under the weight of the tractor tire, the little boy was still miraculously able to run to his father and alert him that he had just been run over.

John Louis was rushed to the hospital, and while in the emergency room, was adamant that the nurses not remove the scapular from around his neck. When they insisted it needed to be removed, he conceded to let them wrap it around his wrist, not letting it leave his body.

He suffered from six broken ribs and seventeen broken bones in his face, including a broken nose. He had bleeding at the back of his head, a collapsed lung, and his organs were malaligned for several days but fortunately drifted back into place with no permanent damage.

The doctors did not have a medical answer to John Louis' absence of pain. With each examination from every specialist on the hospital roster, the miracles grew in number. Everything that should have gone wrong didn't. He should have been killed, but wasn't. He should have been paralyzed, but he walks and runs like a normal, vibrant little boy. His organs should have shut down from being crushed by the heavy weight of the tractor, yet he has no permanent organ damage. He should have lost his eye sight as a result of the crushed bones around his eyes, but his eyes were spared with no damage at all. A handsome little boy, his face is perfectly healed with no sign of trauma. He is truly a walking miracle.

At the tender young age of six, John Louis explained to his mother and father with great wisdom why God allowed him to suffer such an ordeal. He said it was because Jesus wanted him to tell others of the power of the brown scapular and to encourage the faithful to wear it.

What a profound statement of faith by such a young boy. So often, God speaks to us through children because of their purity and receptivity. This little boy knew full well there was no magic trick involved with wearing the brown scapular, nor a contractual agreement of any sort between him and God when he wears his scapular. No, he understands what faith is. He holds tight to it; he wears his faith around his shoulders and in his heart like that suit of armor Grandmother explained to us so well.

So many Christians strive all their lives to achieve a level of knowledge, wisdom, and faith such as his. Childlike faith is what God desires of us, believing in something just because God tells us to.

*"At that time the disciples approached Jesus and said, 'Who is the greatest in the kingdom of Heaven?' He called a child over, placed it in their midst, and said, 'Amen I say to you, unless you turn and become like children, you will not enter the kingdom of Heaven'."*
*Matthew 18:1-3*

Being completely convinced of the validity of the brown scapular through the effects of faith, I too, started wearing the scapular again as an adult. It wasn't until I was doing some dirt work in our yard on a tractor, that I realized as well the power of faith.

I was moving dirt in our yard to create a large flowerbed. The tractor I was using had a history of overturning. In fact, while riding on this tractor, a rancher was tragically killed when it overturned, falling onto him and crushing him. Just as I was heading outside to work on the flowerbeds, I stopped and prayed for God's protection from all harm through the intercession of Mary, His mother. I placed my scapular around my neck and went to work on the tractor.

In the course of moving the dirt, I had to climb on and off the tractor many times while it was still running. After about an hour of this, I was growing tired of climbing up and down the tractor. Without thinking, I reached up, grabbing hold of a pipe to help hoist myself up. As I grabbed the pipe, a bolt of pain surged through me. I fell back onto the ground and realized I had just grabbed the tractor's exhaust pipe. I didn't just touch it, I firmly gripped it, searing my hand. Imagine running your car for an hour and then grabbing the exhaust pipe.

I ran as quickly as I could to the pool area to get my hand into the cool water, but the gate was locked to keep our young children from wandering into the pool. I then frantically tried to get into the house. Coy, however, had a habit of locking the doors during the day whether we were there or not, so unfortunately, I was unable to get into the house.

The minutes rolled by before Coy finally came to unlock the door for me. All I could think about was the need to get my hand on ice. I was certain I would be making a trip to the emergency room with third degree burns.

As I worked feverishly to apply the ice to my hand, I noticed that the burning had stopped. When I looked at my hand I was stunned to find that there was no sign of a burn. It looked just like my other hand that had not been burned. It wasn't even red, only light pink. I knew I should have had whelps and severe burns, but there was nothing.

I remembered immediately the story of my cousin's young son and the brown scapular. I recounted how I had prayerfully placed the scapular around my neck, invoking God's mother for divine protection just before beginning my work on the tractor. I then considered the lesson my grandmother had taught me: *Faith changes everything.*

Three days later, I was beginning to doubt that my miraculous healing was even a miracle at all. While ironing my clothes, I just barely brushed my arm against the warm (not hot) iron. Instantly, my arm formed a huge, painful blister. The pain remained for days, and it took weeks before the scar from brushing up against the warm iron went away. I knew this was God's reminder that yes, my faith did save my hand that day, and that I was granted a great favor through the intercession of Mary and my faithful devotion of wearing the brown scapular.

I know God has provided divine protection for me all of my life. It was by the power of God, through the intercession of His archangel Michael, that my life and Tanner's life were spared in the parking lot that day at the mall. It was my faith that had unleashed that power as I called out to Him. I know God allows His mother to protect His children, and that it was my faith that propelled her protection over me that day on the tractor. If I had thrown the scapular on as a mere good luck charm without the application of faith, I would have been nursing a wounded hand for months; but no, my faith secured me in safety.

*"How numerous, O Lord, my God, You have made your wondrous deeds! And in Your plans for us there is none to equal You. Should I wish to declare them or tell them, too many are they to recount."*

*Psalm 40:6*

# 11

# "I'm Right Here"

My daughter, Ruth Ann, was born in March of 2004. I was overjoyed that God had blessed me with a daughter. I named her after my mother, Ruth, because I knew I would no longer have to yearn for that special mother-daughter relationship I had so desperately longed for with my own mom. Finally, I would have the closeness and the bonding that I lacked. Ruth Ann was God's stamp of approval on my life, and she filled a hollow place in my heart that only a daughter could fill. I couldn't wait to begin to share the things that a mother is supposed to share with a daughter, only my roll had reversed: I wasn't the daughter, I was the mother.

Ruth brought many changes to our home through the years. The boys couldn't understand the emotions and drama that a little girl brings to a household. She was a sweet soul who at cried at the drop of a hat. Coy and her brothers would say, "She's not even hurt. Why is she crying?" I had to remind them that girls don't cry when they get hurt, they cry when their heart hurts. Commercials, sad stories, and sick kittens were the very things that made her cry. She reminded me of myself at her age, because she desperately wanted affirmation that she was loved. Her heart was so pure and simple. I've always said children can see angels because their hearts are pure and their souls aren't soiled with sin.

God has used Ruth Ann's tender heart to deliver so many inspirational messages to me, but none as passionate as the time when she whispered in my ear while I was visiting our Lord during Eucharistic Adoration.

One particular morning, I asked God "What can I do for You today?" This was my ritual, and surprisingly, He answered me clearly each morning. He said to my heart, "Come to Adoration." Knowing that our parish did not offer Eucharistic Adoration on Thursdays, I asked again, "What can I do for you today?" His reply; "Come to Adoration." I knew the Catholic parish in the nearby town held Eucharistic Adoration on Thursdays, so I went.

Ruth Ann was only three years old at the time and was not in school yet, so I brought her with me that day equipped with crayons and a coloring book. She was completely content with coloring while I prayed, "God, here I am." I went on to say, "You know how hard it is for me to hear you in Adoration so please speak clearly to me." I remembered how God had used Cooper to speak to me when he was three, so I specifically requested, "Speak to me through Ruth Ann if you must."

I was kneeling with my head down in prayer and leaning against the back of the pew in front of me when suddenly, I felt Ruth's sweet arms wrap around me. She was standing in the pew in front of me, staring lovingly into my eyes as if she were in a trance. She said very tenderly, "I'm right here." She gazed at me for a moment, hugged me again, and repeated, "I'm right here."

Then, just as if someone had snapped their fingers, she returned to her three-year-old disposition and skipped back to my pew to resume her coloring. I couldn't believe how God had so readily used Ruth to speak volumes to me in those three simple words, *"I'm right here."*

God is always "right here." He knows I just need to be reminded of this sometimes. Not only that, but I must recognize Him and His voice. He has spoken to me through so many different people with whom I have crossed paths but most especially through my own children. There is an art to listening. My hearing is just fine. It's my listening that is impaired most of the time.

So many people have said to me in my lifetime, "I wish I could have moments like yours. You always hear God." My answer is always the same, "You do have moments like those, you just don't recognize them." Their listening, too, might be impaired. God wants to interact with all of us on a daily basis, but if we don't bring Him to the forefront of our thoughts, we lose our sense of awareness that He is right here.

When we are in awareness of Gods daily presence in our lives, it is only then that we can live moment by moment in His marvelous plan. It is in the mundanity and ordinariness of our daily routines that God makes His presence known to us. If we stay alert, we can hear His quiet whisper and see His subtle movements but all too often, it seems like Monday morning rolls around so quickly and I find myself trying to get through the day just so I can get back into bed, only to start over again the next day. But the next day is Tuesday, and what good has Tuesday in store for me? I trudge through Tuesday and can't wait for the day to be over so I can get back into bed in anticipation of the next day, Wednesday. And then there's Wednesday... How easily I become bored with the daily routine of life.

One morning during prayer, just as I was about to take a sip of coffee, it was as if God stopped my hand before I could put the cup to my mouth, and He whispered in my ear, *"Leslie, enjoy the coffee, smell it, taste it, savor it, and then thank Me for it."* His message went on as He told me He wanted me to laugh more and enjoy the life He has given me. He led me to Scripture that morning that spoke about enjoying life. I can't recall which one it was, but throughout the day I encountered many messages reminding me to enjoy the little things in life and laugh more. At least two of my patients came in with T-shirts that read: "Live, Laugh, Love." How embarrassing it is to be so easily bored with the beauty of life that God has to tap me on the shoulder and remind me to be thankful and enjoy what He has given me.

We can find joy if we live for the present day and open our eyes to the good that can be accomplished through our daily, ordinary routine. How many times have I made an impact on a person's life just by doing the everyday activities that are on my many to-do-lists? It is not for us to know how our interactions with others make a difference in their lives. We are just called to remain alert, enjoy life, and be a blessing to others however we can. God puts people in our paths for a reason, but if we trudge through the day, we might miss our opportunities to be a blessing.

I am sure that God uses me for bigger purposes than cleaning teeth when I am at work in the dental office. Nearly every day I notice His hand in my schedule of patients. He either sends me good and holy messages through them, or he prompts me to be a blessing for them outside of anything dental related. One particular patient comes to mind when I reflect how God is very active in my daily interactions with others.

It was at the end of my work day at the dental office, and I was dismissing my last patient in the usual manner. I escorted her to the front desk, where I noticed a little old lady, Miss Clara, at the counter. I noticed she was wearing black shoes that were worn through to her toes. I thought to myself (or the Holy Spirit spoke to me), "She needs a new pair of shoes." I immediately struck up a conversation with her about her shoe size being close to mine. She informed me that she wore a size seven and that those worn-out shoes were the only pair comfortable enough for her to wear. She was discouraged because her daughter had told her that the shoe she had worn nearly all her adult life had been discontinued. It was your typical "old lady" pair of shoes. I asked her the brand name and style of the shoe, and after she left I reviewed her records and copied her mailing address. I was going to buy her those shoes!

When I got home, I quickly logged onto my favorite website and found the exact shoes that Miss Clara was wearing. I was relieved to find out that they had not been discontinued after all, but I was astounded by the price.

They cost one hundred and forty dollars! "Nobody needs a one-hundred-and-forty-dollar pair of shoes!" I thought. I discarded the piece of paper on which I had Clara's mailing address and decided one hundred and forty dollars was just too much to pay for a pair of shoes. Clara would just have to find a different pair of shoes to wear.

After a few moments, my two-year-old son, who was running around the house playing with his brothers, darted over to me with a piece of paper in his hand. It was Miss Clara's mailing address. I took it from him, and while thanking him, I laid the piece of paper down and went about my business. Moments later my two-year-old returned to me, again saying, "Here Mom" as he handed me Miss Clara's address again. I assured him that I didn't need it, but thanked him for bringing it to me.

I took the paper and laid it down once again. A third time, he presented it to me, and it was then that I knew God was using my child, C.J., to deliver a message to me.

I quickly said a prayer: "God, if you want me to buy Clara those shoes, then have C.J. bring her address to me one more time." I folded the paper neatly and set it on the couch where I was sitting. After a short time, I noticed the paper was missing. C.J. was busy playing in the other room with his older brothers. I waited patiently, and after a few moments C.J. rounded the corner, and for the fourth time, he very purposefully handed me the piece of scrap paper containing Miss Clara's address.

Knowing this was no coincidence, I jumped up and went to the computer to buy Miss Clara a new pair of one hundred and forty dollar shoes! Remembering Clara wore a size seven, I chose her size. I was immediately alerted that the only size available was seven, and there was only one pair left in stock. BINGO! I chose the size seven and was then prompted by the computer to choose the proper width. Hmm…medium? I clicked medium width, but the computer would not register my entry. It did absolutely nothing. It didn't ding, or ring, or make that funny noise the computer makes when you hit the wrong button. Click, click, click again, but still nothing. I simply was not allowed to choose medium width, so I figured she must need a different width. It was understandable that Clara might have a narrow foot, being that she was long and lanky in stature. So, I chose narrow width. The computer liked that choice and alerted me that there was only one pair left in stock!

I purchased the size seven shoes with a narrow width and had the company send them straight to Miss Clara's doorstep. After I had completed the ordering process, I started to wonder what she would think about receiving a gift from a strange company off eBay, so I checked the name of the seller, only to be reassured even more that it was God's hand guiding me. The eBay seller was "Faith, Hope and Love." I knew Clara would be thrilled to receive her new shoes from "Faith, Hope and Love."

God gives each of us opportunities to serve Him and others every day. We just need to be able to recognize them. My sister will occasionally comment that she fears she will only enter heaven by the skin of her teeth, because rarely does it occur to her to serve others through charitable works. She is most comfortable in the background of life, whereas I like front and center stage. She has mentioned that I must have a mansion waiting in heaven for me because of all the service and volunteer work I do for the community, and that she just hopes God has a tiny hut waiting for her in heaven. She says a hut will be just fine, as long as she's in heaven. I can't help but think how the opposite must be true. Her service is subtle and unnoticed; therefore, all of her accolades will be in heaven, while my service is mostly noisy and loud, and I receive my applause here on earth. She just might be surprised at the mansion waiting for her.

Everyone has some God-given talent to use to bring others to Christ, and Sondra has plenty of them. Sondra was gifted with a sharp mind and unrelenting determination like no one else I know. She is strong as an ox, even at age 49 (and holding). When we have a workday at our family ranch, she hauls things in her two arms like a mule. I, on the other hand, am basically the cheerleader, letting her know how good she is doing.

I view farm work as something that gets you really smelly and dirty. Let's not forget about the spiders, and scorpions, and snakes. I like to leave that sort of work for the men or my grown sons. Sondra never chastises me, though. She understands our differences and takes pride in knowing that she is the queen of physical hard work, and I'm content to let her be queen for the day. Her God-given talents are her relentless stamina, strength, and her willingness to get dirty.

I guess I expect everyone to be noisy about their service to God. Being in the spotlight, however, is not what service is supposed to be about, yet I tend to desire it. I know that God gave me this desire because He wishes for me to use it to serve Him. Not everyone can be in the spotlight, nor does everyone desire it. Some people are satisfied with staying behind the scenes. Our individualities define what sort of service God is calling us to. It takes all sorts of personalities and all sorts of service to get "all the bases covered."

It's like the story of the two men who recited Psalm 23 to a coliseum full of people. Each man delivered the psalm within the boundary of their own persona and countenance as he spoke the following words:

> *"The Lord is my Shepherd; I shall not want. He makes me to lie down in green pastures; He leads me beside the still waters. He restores my soul. He leads me in the path of righteousness for His name sake. Yea, though I walk through the shadow of death, I will fear no evil for Thou are with me. Thy rod and staff they comfort me. Thou prepare a table before me in the presence of my enemies. Thou anoint my head with oil, my cup overflows. Surely goodness and mercy will follow me all the days of my life and I will dwell in the house of the Lord forever."*

The first speaker was a young, vibrant man full of energy and charisma. He knew the psalm well and delivered it powerfully with bold fervor. The audience roared and cheered at such a wonderful presentation. The man was well pleased with his delivery and the standing ovation granted him.

The second man was old and soft spoken. When it was his turn to speak, he tenderly spoke the words of the psalm with heartfelt meaning, as if no one was in the room except he and the Lord. When he finished, not a word was spoken. No cheers or applause was granted him. The room was dead silent. Deeply moved by the words of the second speaker, the first speaker addressed the audience, saying, "I may know the psalm... but he knows the shepherd."[5]

Many people, like my sister, are serving others, just much more quietly than I. Their style, like hers, is just different from mine. One of the best things Sondra does for God on a daily basis, besides her vocation as wife and mother, is show compassion to a five-year-old boy who lives in a disturbing home next door to her. His name is Edward. Edward is starved for attention. He longs for security and love. Sondra allows this troubled child to spend time in her home every single day. She feeds him healthy meals and showers him with love and respect through her motherly discipline. Her children tolerate his intrusion and play well with him. She is a beacon for this little boy who may not see the light of Christ anywhere else. She doesn't always enjoy the extra mouth to feed or the extra person to clean up after, but she understands that God put Edward in her life so that she could nurture and care for him and lead him to Christ.

There are many opportunities to serve God through our ministry to others throughout our daily lives. We need only open our eyes and see what is right in front of us.

# 12

# The Heart of the Matter

Once in confession, I was complaining about "stupid people" and how I couldn't stand to be around them. I went on to confess that I really didn't like very many people because they got on my nerves. Really, my struggle was with myself. Actually, I was more frustrated with my own failure to love others with their weaknesses and faults than I was with the fault itself. I am so easily annoyed when I witness mediocrity that I end up in sin from the chastisements that come from my mouth. I would consider it a great victory one day if I could just simply think someone is an idiot, rather than saying it! Ugh, baby steps.

After my lengthy confession and self-condemnation, the priest simply replied, "That's your cross to bear." I answered him saying, "That's just it, Father. I don't think I have a cross, compared to some of the crosses other people have to bear, and yet, I am so quick to complain." He just looked at me, smiled, and said, "Oh, you have a cross all right; it's your personality!"

Aha! I finally reached the heart of the matter—my heart! He went on to explain that my cross was living with myself. My cross was the perfectionist in me. I started thinking about who gets on my nerves the most, and well, the answer was ME. He said my "perfectionist" personality makes life hard because it is difficult for me to live up to my own standards one hundred percent of the time and nearly impossible for others to live according to the standards I have set. He did not suggest that perfection is unattainable. It is something to strive for as long as we are striving for perfection in Christ.

Perfection comes with sacrifice. Perfection comes with desiring to be less. Perfection comes when we take our focus off of ourselves. Perfection comes when we desire God's character… and nothing less.

Once I realized the problem with my temperament was me and not other people, I was able to reassess how I should interact with others. I decided no interaction was best—that way I would remain "safe." I started avoiding situations where I knew I was going to be around a lot of people that would annoy me. I tried to abstain from gossip and parties where I knew there would be a lot of women present. I have found that going to a party with a lot of other women is like entering into a henhouse. When there are many hens around, there is lots of clucking—providing many occasions to sin. It never fails; once I have said something very "Leslie," the hens in the henhouse start squawking and feathers get ruffled.

———

*"Create in me a clean heart O God."*
*Psalm 51:10*

———

I started to drift toward like-minded people of faith. This is where I feel the most comfortable. While avoiding occasions of sin, is certainly helpful, it isn't the solution. It is merely sticking my head in the sand. It doesn't help me overcome my sinful tendencies; it only helps me avoid them. I can't run from certain people all of my life—like a fugitive trying not to get caught in a sticky situation; I have to change within.

I ask God regularly to show me my sins and to make me hate them so much that I will avoid them at all costs and eventually overcome them. He lets me know exactly what my sins are and always provides a way for me to conquer them. But it is never easy, in fact, it is excruciatingly difficult. Why is a change of heart so difficult? Well, basically, the answer is pride. This I know for sure; my heart is the matter. Our hearts are *always* the matter.

———

*"More torturous than all else is the human heart,*
*beyond remedy; who can understand it? I, the Lord,*
*alone probe the mind and test the heart…"*
*Jeremiah 17:9-10*

———

Just after receiving the Eucharist during Holy Mass, I knelt in prayer and asked God to show me my sins. Just then, my eyes were diverted to a really nice pair of boots walking up the aisle to Communion. "Oh, cute boots," I thought. Then, my eyes were drawn upward, and there it was: my sin!

The woman wearing those boots was the very source of my sins. I had been so sickened by this woman's lack of obedience in her duty to her children and husband through her sin of adultery that I brought myself to sin by dwelling on hers. The Lord reminded me that I should be very careful not to be lured into the sin of throwing stones.

Booker T. Washington once said:

> *"I will not permit any man to narrow and degrade my soul by making me hate him."*

I was focusing on her sin, and by doing so, I was heaping upon my own heart a sin even greater than hers.

Tolerance of sin is sin in itself. We are not called to be tolerant of sin, but we are called to be tolerant of the sinner. Being human is really tough, but no sin is worth giving away our salvation. I will not, and cannot, accept the sins of society that have become acceptable. I'm not going to hell for anyone by agreeing with sin just so others can feel comfortable in society, wrapped in their sin like an expensive fur to be proud of and flaunted before others.

Jesus commands us to love others as we love ourselves. Therefore, if we love others, we will not condone sin nor acknowledge sin as anything less than it is. We must not approve of lifestyles or choices of which God disapproves. We are called to lovingly accept the sinner while always striving to be an ambassador for good and moral living. This is what Christ calls each one of us to do so that we can draw others into the light.

My stepmother once said to me, "Leslie, you just have a strong personality that is hard to like." I didn't quite know how to reply to her statement. I just know God gave me this "full throttle" personality for a reason. How I choose to live out my individuality is my choice to make. I want to live for Christ, so therefore, I must use my personality to draw others to Him and not run them off. I am constantly searching for gentleness because I know God wants me to possess it. Gentleness is the governor, or the brake if you will, that sets our countenance in line with God's countenance. It is a treasure to own, I'm sure, but I have yet to acquire it.

# 13

# Remember the Crepe Myrtles

Moment by moment God calls us to lean on Him and let Him bless our daily choices, which means relying on Him for everything, even the small stuff. When I hand over my entire day to the Lord, I find that my time is well spent and everything falls nicely into place. I try to make a habit of including Jesus in all of my daily decisions. Even where to go to get a good bargain!

The time had come to pull out the four Blue Point Juniper trees in the front of our house. They were dying from the top down and needed to be replaced. I knew I wanted to replace them with pink, flowering crepe myrtles. Worried, however, about the expense of buying four nice-sized crepe myrtle trees, I asked Jesus to help me find some crepe myrtles—CHEAP. I know praying for a good bargain might seem odd, but if we can't rely on God for the small stuff, how then will we ever learn to trust Him with the "big" stuff?

The morning I set out to buy the trees, I again asked God to direct my path to just the right place to find beautiful crepe myrtles. Knowing full well He hears all of my prayers and is delighted to take complete control of every aspect of my life, I set out to a homebuilder's store forty-five minutes away because they have a nice garden center there. When I told my friend where I was going, her reply was, "Do they have crepe myrtles? "I'm not sure. I just know that is where I am supposed to go," I answered. I just had that gut instinct that I get when the Holy Spirit is guiding me. So, I was off!

When I arrived at the garden center, I made a quick pass through it but didn't find any crepe myrtles. So, I asked the attendant whether they had any in stock. She quickly said, "No, we don't have any at this time." I wasn't going to settle for that, so I searched still longer. Coming upon another sales clerk, I posed the same question, only to get the same answer, "Sorry, no."

Convinced I was at the right place for crepe myrtles, I waited a few more minutes until I saw a third sales person. I approached her and said, "I am looking for crepe myrtle trees and I need about four. Do you have any?" She responded, "No…." then paused for a moment and said, "Well, I do have some stuck away in the back. We're not supposed to sell them, because we just sprayed them for bugs, but…I can sell them to you at seventy-five percent off their original price."

Jackpot! I knew there was a prize in store for me that day. She took me to a small area away from the garden center where there were several beautiful, pink, flowering crepe myrtles trees. I chose my four trees and purchased them for only three dollars each. God is GOOD. I thanked God and all the way home I thought about how remarkable it is that He cares about every tiny detail of my life, not just the big stuff.

So many times, we fail to ask for God's intercession because we tend to think our wants or needs are insignificant. It is so easy to say we have faith when faced with trials in our lives but lose all faith or just simply refuse to call on God for the easy stuff. We always hear the message "Nothing is too big for God," but we forget that nothing is too small for Him either. Scripture tells us over and over again...

*"With God all things are possible."*
*Matthew 19:26*

Notice it says "ALL things," not just "important" things, but *all* things. He doesn't have to work any harder to cure us from disease than He does to solve our everyday dilemmas—like where to go to get cheap crepe myrtles.

It is by factoring faith into the "silly," insignificant moments of our lives that we become spiritually mature so that, eventually, we are stable enough to hand God the really big and scary stuff with ease and inner peace. Sometimes when I start to worry about future things such as finances, illness and even death, I whisper to myself, "Remember the crepe myrtles."

# Part Two

# Solid Food

*"Although you should be teachers by this time,
you need to have someone teach you again the
basic elements of the utterances of God.  You need
milk and not solid food.  Everyone who lives on
milk lacks experience of the word of righteousness,
for he is a child.  But solid food is for the
mature, for those whose faculties are trained by
practice to discern good and evil."*

*Hebrews 5:12-14*

# 14

# The Summons

Asking God to guide me each day and reveal to me
what He wants from me is rather easy. The tough
part is doing what He asks of me. Why should I even bother
asking if I am not going to put forth any effort to obey?

So many times, God has called me to prayer and
Adoration. I didn't do particularly well in Eucharistic
Adoration because I would either fall asleep or my mind
would wander. The distraction of others would also
contribute to my inattentiveness. So, I did not attend
Adoration on a regular basis. All the while, however, the
Lord kept calling me to Him through our morning meetings
or through others. Yet, even as numerous people encouraged
me to attend Adoration, I went only occasionally. I knew
God was serious and was tired of begging me when I was in
line at the meat market, waiting for the butcher to help me

with my order.

I watched the butcher greet each customer before me, "Good evening, what can I get for you today?" The next customer in line received a similar greeting, "How can I help you today?" When it was finally my turn to give my order to the butcher, he looked at me, and instead of his usual greeting, he said very clearly, "Have you been to Adoration today?" Stunned, I said, "No," and his reply was, "We're open till nine." (Adoration ran until nine that evening.) He then looked past me to the next customer standing in line behind me, and said, "Hi there. What can I get for you this evening?" I never did get my meat order, but I got my orders, I was sure of that. To Adoration I went.

It is not what we "achieve" in Adoration that pleases God; it is our simple willingness to be in His presence that pleases Him. I struggled in Adoration because I did not sense His presence. I felt like I couldn't accomplish anything by being there, but God wasn't asking me to accomplish anything. He was simply calling me to sit with Him and be silent.

I must be careful that my time spent in the Lord's presence doesn't become a task or work. It is when I am in His presence that I feel at peace and at rest. Nothing needs to get done; just giving my time to the Lord is enough. Many times, during Adoration, I nod off to sleep. I know God is okay with this because He wants me to be completely relaxed in His presence.

I have to remember not to make things harder than they need to be. When God calls us to prayer, we need to view that calling as an invitation to spend time at the most luxurious and relaxing spa in town. He wants us to just relax and sit face to face with Him, handing everything over to His care. Nothing is demanded of us. We just need to be still, and if need be, nod off.

---

*"Be still, and know that I am God."*

*Psalm 46:10*

---

I am embarrassed to admit that even after receiving my orders from the butcher that day, I soon drifted away from spending time in Adoration. I was a very busy mom with lots of things that needed to get done. I worked at the dental office during the day, and when I turned forty, I added another work load to my already hectic schedule. I opened a dance studio and began teaching dance and fitness classes in the evenings. God, however, was not going to let me place Him on the back burner, and He went to even greater lengths in summoning me to prayer and Adoration. He was not going to take "no" for an answer. God has a great sense of adventure, and what a well-orchestrated adventure we went on! And it all started with a box of chocolates.

It was nearing the Christmas holiday, and at the end of my ballet class one of my students gave me a box of chocolates. I was excited about the chocolates because I loved receiving gifts, and if they contained chocolate, even better! I couldn't wait to get home to enjoy my chocolate treat. After biting into one of the chocolates, however, I was disappointed to find caramel in the middle. What a perfect way to ruin a good piece of chocolate, putting caramel in the middle! I sampled each piece of chocolate hoping to find one without caramel, but to no avail. All had caramel centers.

I was disappointed about the wasted box of chocolates—it was a bad night.

Here is where the story about the caramel centered chocolates gets interesting. The next day when I was heading to the shopping mall to get some last-minute Christmas gifts, I turned my radio to the Catholic station and heard these words; "So, what is Caramel?" I am sure my head jerked and looked at the radio to make sure I heard what I thought I heard. The speaker's next words were, "Well basically, it is prayer." He then proceeded to explain the devotion of the Carmelite nuns, who commit their lives to prayer. "Well, isn't that a coincidence?" I thought.

I arrived at the mall, and after a few hours of searching for those hard to find gifts, I finished my shopping. When I started the car to go home, a different talk show was being aired on the radio, and the first words that came across my car speakers were, "Be fervent in your prayer." I knew that I was receiving small messages from God and that He was calling me to prayer. I was pleased with God's creative ingenuity with the whole caramel candy thing and the Carmelite nun story and how it was all tied to prayer. I must not have been motivated to the degree God was calling me to be, however, so the saga with caramel continued.

When I arrived home that afternoon, I picked up the kids from school and my oldest son, Cooper, was excited to show me two gaping holes in his mouth where he had two less teeth than he had when he left for school that morning. "Hey, Mom, I lost two baby molars at school today," he exclaimed. I asked him how he lost two molars in one day, and he said, "Someone gave me a caramel and when I bit down on it, it pulled out my loose teeth." A caramel? "Again with the caramels," I thought. My mind started reeling about the influx of caramels the past two days. I thought about what the speaker had said about the meaning of Caramel and the devotions of the Carmelite nuns to prayer. I knew this was surely a sign from God that He wanted me to pray more. I decided I was going to spend more time in prayer, but I just needed to get a lot of other things done first.

On day three I was pondering the whole caramel thing. I thought about how I could go a whole year or more without ever encountering a silly caramel, but in the past two days I had been bombarded with them. Still, I kept busy with menial tasks, as if I were running from God. I even found myself cleaning out the spare tire compartment of my car. Who does that? I was really avoiding God! As I pulled out my spare tire, low and behold, I saw it: a single caramel still in its wrapping. After staring at the caramel for a moment like a deer stares into the headlights of an oncoming car, I conceded and drove straight to Adoration and I got down on my knees in prayer!

Again, it was as if God needed to hit me over the head with a two-by-four to get my attention. What was I afraid of? Maybe I didn't think I had anything significant to pray about. God longed for me to be with Him. He wasn't requiring me to have some profound well scripted prayer, He just missed me and He wanted me to spend time with Him.

Subconsciously, I was excluding Him. Even though I was a prayerful woman, God was, and is constantly drawing me into a deeper understanding of Him through quality time spent together. God is relentless. He won't accept anything less than our undying attention, because He loves us so much.

# 15

# Believe

Each moment we spend with God we fertilize our garden and we grow in the gifts of the Holy Spirit. Through the seven gifts of the Holy Spirit, we are able to have an elevated understanding of our loving Father. The gifts of the Spirit bring forth fruit, but each in its proper order. The gifts must come first while the fruit is a result of owning the gift.

> *The seven gifts of the Holy Spirit are permanent supernatural qualities that enable the graced person to be especially in tune with the inspirations of the Holy Spirit. These gifts make us holy. They are **wisdom**; which helps a person value the things of heaven, **understanding**; which enables the person to grasp the truths of religion, **counsel**; which*

*helps one see and correctly choose the best practical approach in serving God,* **fortitude***; which steels a person's resolve in overcoming obstacles to living the faith,* **knowledge***; which helps one see the path to follow and the dangers to one's faith,* **piety***; which fills a person with confidence in God and an eagerness to serve Him, and* **fear of the Lord***; which makes a person keenly aware of God's sovereignty and the respect due to Him and His laws.*[6]

Once we own the gifts of the Spirit, we are able to hear God's voice with intelligibility. Naturally, without effort, we are then able to apply that intelligence to our thought process and decision making. We are enlightened beyond our own reasoning and are enabled to see the Truth more clearly than ever before. When we earnestly pray for the gifts of the Spirit, God places each gift into our hearts and we are transformed to the core of our being. It is only then that God can reveal things beyond reason to us, and we are made to understand through His divine providence. It is then when we are able to bear fruit.

————

*"But the fruit of the Spirit is love, joy, peace, patience, kindness, generosity, faithfulness, gentleness, self-control."*
*Galatians 5:22-23*

————

In order to bear good fruit, God requires us to have receptivity to Him. As we grow in our understanding of Him, and learn to trust His voice within our souls, we must be receptive to that voice.

During Holy Mass one Sunday, God revealed His supernatural existence in the Eucharist in such an awe-inspiring way that it changed my life. The roots of my faith were strengthened as God pointed out my disbelief in the physical presence of Jesus that, through the power of the Holy Spirit, is made real in the form of bread and wine at Holy Sacrifice of the Mass. Even though I professed to believe, God showed me my weakness and placed the gifts of His Spirit within me in full measure—beyond my limited capacity of understanding.

Receiving Jesus' body and blood in the Eucharist is the center focus of the Catholic Mass. But I took God's tremendous gift of Himself for granted. My lackadaisical approach to receiving Jesus in Holy Communion was substandard for any good Catholic. I went through the motions without any regard to the enormity of the gift of being able to receive Jesus—to actually ingest Him into my body each week through the Sacrament of Holy Communion.

Here is where my Protestant friends might want to shut the book, or at the very least skip to the next chapter, but I challenge you to keep reading. If nothing in this next section is true, then you have nothing to lose by reading it, but what if it is true? Just think what you have to gain…

One Sunday, after receiving the host (the Body of Christ), I bypassed drinking from the cup of wine that follows (the Blood of Christ). Being a dental hygienist, I am very aware of germs and how cross-contamination works. I had bypassed the Precious Blood of Christ at Mass for years because I did not want to drink after all of the other parishioners who drank from the cup before me. After passing up the cup of His Precious Blood, I knelt down in prayer and heard very distinctly, *"Leslie, don't you believe?"* God spoke directly to my heart. He sounded so disappointed and wounded by my disbelief.

Immediately, I was overcome with sorrow and repented, mortified by my severe lack of faith. God revealed to me, *"Nothing impure can ever touch the Living God."*

If I believed in His presence in the bread, why then, would the same not be true for the wine? I was enlightened with the Truth that nothing impure could ever defile Jesus or the vessel that contains Him. He opened my eyes and heart to the profound, unexplainable Truth of His Real Presence—body, blood, soul, and divinity—at each and every Mass through the consecration of the bread and wine.

I know now, without a shadow of a doubt, that nothing is greater than He—not disease, nor the flu, nor anything vile. I am so convicted of this that I would be happy to drink the last drop of the Blood of Christ left in the bottom of the cup, even after the most highly contagious individual had drunk from it before me.

When Jesus healed the leper, He didn't just heal him with a word, He healed him with His touch. The leper's highly contagious disease couldn't defile our Lord because He is GOD. Germs can't defile the cup of His blood, because we know that its contents are no longer ordinary wine, but through the Sacrifice of the Mass have become Jesus' very blood. Jesus made this very clear to His disciples. He was adamant that they eat His flesh and drink His blood. It is a mystery to us as to why He wants this of us, but He requires us to trust Him and have faith in Him. He knows our humanness and shields our eyes from the actual transformation that takes place, because He knows how hard it would be for us to actually eat human flesh and drink human blood if we could see it. Also, God puts a veil over our eyes, not permitting us to see His Real Presence, because He wants us to have FAITH.

Many disciples deserted Jesus the day He instructed them to eat His flesh and drink His blood, but He didn't call them back, because He knew they fully understood what He was asking them to do. Had they misunderstood Him, Jesus would have called them back and clarified to them that He only meant they were to eat His flesh and drink His blood *figuratively*. That would have been a lot easier to accept, because it is more agreeable with our human thinking. Jesus, however, did not do that. God wants us to have faith in Him and believe that what He asks of us through the Eucharist is for our good, even though we don't comprehend it.

---

*"Many of His disciples who were listening said, 'This is hard; who can accept it?...Jesus knew that His disciples were murmuring about this, and He said to them, 'Does this shock you?...The words I have spoken to you are spirit and life but there are some of you who do not believe.' Jesus knew from the beginning the ones who would not believe. As a result of this, many disciples returned to their former way of life and no longer accompanied Him."*
*John 6:60-61, 63-64, 66*

In the original Greek translation, Jesus' instructions to His disciples to eat His flesh, the word for "eats" (tragon) actually means to "tear off and chew." Those deserters knew exactly what Jesus was asking of them, and freely chose against it. The same is true for the disciples who stayed. They, too, knew exactly what Jesus was commanding them to do. As absurd as it may have seemed, they put their faith in the One whom they knew could bring them to everlasting life.

About a year after I had this experience at Mass, I was chosen to be the director of a women's Catholic spiritual retreat in a nearby parish. As director, one of my duties was to give an inspirational talk to a group of about eighty women about the significance of the Seven Sacraments of the Catholic Church: Baptism, Confirmation, Reconciliation, the Eucharist, Marriage, Anointing of the Sick, and Holy Orders (becoming a priest), and The Last Rites. When I spoke about the Sacrament of the Eucharist, the Holy Spirit guided my words very carefully. I explained my former weakness of faith in the Real Presence of our Lord through the consecration of the bread and wine at Holy Mass. I recounted my story of that unforgettable moment during Mass when God opened my eyes to my fault of disbelief. The women listened intently as I repeated the words that Jesus spoke to me that day, *"Leslie, don't you believe?"* I urged them to put aside their fears and to just believe.

After my lengthy and emotional talk, I was approached by one tearful woman after another. They told me how they, too, were reluctant to drink after others because of their blindness to the Truth. I was humbled that God saw fit to use me—the weakest of all, to bring about so many conversions of heart. God used my weakness to glorify Him.

After the three days of our spiritual retreat we returned to Saint Peter's Parish for Sunday morning Mass. The priest had never before witnessed what happened that morning during Communion. Both sides of the aisles where the cup of Christ's blood was being offered were at a standstill. Every single woman who had been on that retreat stood in line awaiting the Blood of Christ. The front of the church looked like a traffic jam on Interstate Highway 35. I thought surely the Precious Blood was going to run out, but just like the story of the loaves and fishes, there was enough for every single person to drink from the cup.

During cold and flu season one year, it was announced that, by the order of the Bishop, some parishes were removing the cup of Precious Blood from the Mass so as to not spread the flu virus. I had vehemently instilled my belief in the Real Presence of Christ in my children each time they went to Mass. I had instructed them to never pass up the cup of Christ's Precious Blood and to simply believe with all of their hearts in the Truth of the transformation of the bread into Jesus' body and the wine into Jesus' blood. So, when came announcement of the removal of the cup because of flu season, I couldn't believe my ears! I was so saddened by this that I went to talk with a priest to gain a better understanding of the issue. I explained that I was upset that we were led to believe that germs could somehow be spread through sharing the cup of Jesus' blood. I remember the priest saying to me, "Leslie, you can't stick your hand in the toilet and then touch the consecrated host and not defile it." My answer to him was, "Yes, I can! Nothing impure can live on Jesus." He just looked at me and smiled as if I had just passed a test and said, "That is your faith."

The Catholic Church's understanding of the Eucharist is so profound that until the Second Vatican council in the 1960s, the faithful only received the consecrated host on the tongue while kneeling. Like baby birds holding their beaks open waiting to be fed, the faithful of the Church opened their mouths while the priest placed the host on their tongue. The host was so revered that no one was allowed to touch it except for the priest in fear that the host might crumble and parts of it fall to the floor and be discarded. Something so blessed and holy should be treated with the utmost respect.

Not long ago a man was visiting our church and went up to receive the Eucharist during Mass. Because of his behavior while trying to receive the host, I suspect he was not Catholic and did not understand the true meaning of the Eucharist. When the priest held up the host and recited the words, "The Body of Christ," the man tried to "take" it from the priest. But the priest kept pulling it back from him, because we are not supposed to "take" Jesus, we are to receive Him. After two or three attempts, the priest instructed the visitor to simply hold out his hand so that the host could be placed there. The Eucharist is to be received on the tongue or in the palm of our hands as a gift from the priest, who is the sacramental representative of Christ.

I have tried to teach my children the importance of faith and of trusting while not comprehending the mystery of the Eucharist. It takes faith to drink from a cup after several hundred other people have drunk from it. So many good Catholics easily fall into the mindset that the consecrated bread and wine are merely symbols of Christ. Protestant religions embrace the symbolic nature of the bread and wine.

Some years ago, the American people were bum-foozled

into thinking that artificial substitutes were somehow better for us to consume than the natural foods we had been eating. We were introduced to fake butters and artificial sweeteners. According to the advertising, the consumer would never be able to tell the difference, for example, between margarine and real butter. Like a bunch of dumb sheep, we all jumped off the cliff and canon-balled into a big ravine of hydrogenated oil. It tasted somewhat the same as the real thing and looked like the real thing, but was a mere imitation of the real thing. The imitations, however, did not nourish our bodies the way the natural predecessors did. Over the years our bodies began suffering from the onslaught of unnatural "foods" (for lack of a better word). If we don't give our bodies the nourishment that is required for us to sustain life, we slowly get sick. Nothing rings truer than that of the Real Presence of Christ in the Eucharist. If we don't give our bodies the nourishment of Christ Himself, our souls slowly get sick.

There is undeniable scientific proof of the Real Presence of Jesus in the Eucharist. The true story of the miracle of Lanciano, Italy, tells of an eighth-century priest who, at the moment of the consecration of the bread and wine, was tempted to doubt the Real Presence of Christ in the bread and wine. Before his eyes, the host turned into real living flesh and the wine into real blood. The blood coagulated into five small clots, all different in form and size.

Four authentications have been performed throughout the centuries on the flesh and blood, the latest being in the 1970s. At that time, by order of the Holy See, the most scientifically complete test was run on the flesh and blood. Microscopic studies found that the flesh was real, living human flesh and composed of cardiac muscular tissue. No preservatives were detected. It remains today, 100 percent natural, living flesh without the use of preservatives, even after over one thousand years of existence. Both the flesh and blood are of the same blood type, AB. The blood contains the proper amount of proteins found in normal fresh blood.[7]

———————

*"Amen, amen I say to you: Unless you eat the flesh of the Son of Man, and drink His blood, you shall not have life within you. Whoever eats My flesh and drinks My blood has everlasting life, and I will raise him up on the last day. For My flesh is true food, and My blood is true drink. Whoever eats My flesh and drinks My blood remains in Me and I in him."*

*John 6:53-54*

———————

# 16

# The Search

Through baptism we are given a set of keys. These keys are in our possession throughout our lifetime. They are the keys to heaven. Some of us search for our keys frantically, when all along they are right in the palm of our hands. We look away from Jesus to other idols and lose sight of our keys. Sometimes we just need someone to help us find them again, a different pair of eyes looking with us. How many times have I misplaced my keys and searched my purse throughout, only to find them right where I had left them. Through our participation of the Mass and Holy Communion, we have our keys in hand.

Through baptism, God our Father entrusts the keys of heaven to each one of us. Sometimes we try to fit them into different doors. The only door they will fit into is Jesus. No matter how hard we push and torque them, they simply won't fit into any other "keyhole" than Jesus.

Remember the old game show "Let's make a Deal?" I remember it well. Contestants were given the chance to choose door number one, door number two, or door number three for a grand prize. The grand prize was only behind one door, so they had to choose by randomly guessing where they hoped the prize would be. Sometimes they would hit the jackpot and win a new car or something of that nature, but other times there was a stinky goat waiting for them behind the door. Jesus is the door where our true grand prize is hidden.

In a wonderful book by Charles L. Allen, *God's Psychiatry*, He writes:

> *Once a young man came to Buddha seeking the true way of life; the path of deliverance. According to the story, as Dr. Ralph Sockman tells it, Buddha led him down to the river. The young man assumed that he was to undergo some ritual of purification, some type of baptismal service. They walked out into the river for some distance and Buddha suddenly grabbed the man and held his head under the water. Finally in a last gasp, the fellow wrenched himself loose, and his head came above the water. Quietly, Buddha asked him. 'When you thought you were drowning, what did you desire most?' The man gasped, 'Air.' Back came Buddha's reply, 'When you want salvation as much as you wanted air, then you will get it.'* [8]

It is important to note there is a fundamental difference between Buddha and Jesus. The difference being;

*With Buddha, "salvation" is achieved. In Jesus, salvation is received.*

Buddha's philosophy was such that "salvation" is something you must work out on your own. Your debt must be paid by you, therefore, your "salvation" comes from yourself.

In Jesus, salvation is a gift. There is nothing humanly possible that we can do to deserve or earn our way to heaven. It is ours if we only accept Jesus. It was through Jesus that God bore the weight of our sins by assuming all of humanity's debt, and ultimately, paid the price for our salvation: His crucifixion. The debt has been paid.

---

*"Who, though He was in the form of God, did not regard equality with God something to be grasped. Rather, He emptied Himself, taking the form of a slave, coming in human likeness, and found human in appearance, He humbled Himself becoming obedient to death, even death on a cross. Because of this, God greatly exalted Him and bestowed on Him the name that is above every other name, that at the name of Jesus, every knee should bend, of those in heaven and on earth and under the earth, and every tongue confess that Jesus Christ is Lord to the glory of God the Father."*
*Philippians 2:6-11*

Since we are all created in the image of Christ who is
perfect, our perfection comes through Christ. No human
being can seek and successfully find enlightenment through
self. Although we are made in God's image, His infinite
knowledge and wisdom is beyond our reach. God is superior
and we are inferior. There are limitations that come with our
humanness. God purposely designed us in this way, for if we
had the mind of God, we wouldn't need faith.

*"For My thoughts are not your thoughts, and My
ways are not your ways, says the Lord. As high as the
heavens are above the earth, so high are My ways
above your ways and My thoughts above
your thoughts."*
*Isaiah 55:8-9*

Buddha, realizing he was not God, never claimed to
be God—since he did not believe in God. Yet, he sought
understanding of "god" with all of his heart, mind, and
soul. Every single human being is created for this purpose,
to seek his maker: God. But what we seek, we must first
believe exists.

*"For anyone who approaches God must believe that
He exists and that He rewards those who seek Him."*
*Hebrews 11:6*

Jesus Christ did not have to seek enlightenment or
perfection, because He was, and is perfection. He is God.

He knows it, has always known it, and proclaimed it.

The point of the story is this: Jesus wants us to hunger and thirst for Him. He wants us to desire salvation like a drowning person gasping for air. If we desire salvation more than anything, that very desire makes an impact on our lives. It forms our inner most being and changes the way we think and act.

Like Buddha, we ought to search unceasingly for knowledge and Truth. God loves His creation so well, that He was willing to come into the world and take on human form, Jesus. When we find the Truth, we find Jesus. When we find Jesus, we find God, because the two are one. Like the very air we breathe, we cannot have life without it, so too, we cannot have eternal life without Jesus.

The longing in our hearts for good things such as nature, love, happiness, home, family, and beauty is the rubber band that holds us connected to our Maker. All good and wonderful things are evidence of our Creator and should be embraced and sought out. Saying "yes" to the good desires of our hearts makes us complete, because it is God Himself who places those yearnings deep within us.

When I think of how much God yearns for us to know Him and love Him, I am reminded of a popular song, "I Want You to Want Me" by the band, "Cheap Trick." The lyrics are so simple, yet ingenious! When I hear the lyrics, I envision Jesus Himself saying them, "I want you to want Me, I need you to need Me, I'd love you to love Me."

Nothing is more desperate than a father's search for his children who are lost. With the same intensity of love, God so longs for each of us to know Him as our loving Father that He will stop at nothing to bring us home to Him. I can imagine a child that has gone missing and God searching and never giving up until that child is safely home.

I gave a similar analogy to my twelve-year-old nephew who had not yet been baptized, except I reversed the roles for him to understand my point better. I told him a story about a missing father, and a child's search...

I questioned my nephew as to when he was going to consider baptism. When he just gave a shrug, I explained to him that baptism says "yes" to Jesus and opens the door to heaven for him. He still seemed disinterested, so I tried to speak in terms that he would understand.

I said to him, "What if one day your dad left for work and never came back and every day you waited at the curb with your heart aching because your dad was not coming home to you? As you waited, you wondered whether his absence meant that he had stopped loving you. That would be unbearable for you, wouldn't it?" I explained the same is true for Jesus. "Jesus is waiting in agony over you. He patiently longs for you to come home to Him."

My nephew remained quiet for a while and I don't know whether anything I had said sank in. I just hope I planted a seed that will eventually mature in him and help him choose Christ through baptism. He needs a set of keys.

I was given a chance to feel the pain a parent feels when her child has gone missing. It is one of the worst experiences a parent can ever undergo.

When my daughter, Ruth, was eight years old, our family went on vacation to a large resort near Austin. It had many buildings with multiple levels and lots of entertainment areas for the kids. After we had been staying there nearly a week, it was time to pack up and go home. Ruth wanted a last-minute snack before we left and asked whether she could go by herself to the snack area. My gut instinct screamed out, "NO! Go with her." The snack area was an elevator ride down three floors, a trek across the grounds, up another elevator and through a long corridor. I was so lazy that I let her convince me that she could go it alone. What sort of mother was I? After about thirty minutes Ruth had not returned so we sent her brothers on a search and rescue mission. Another thirty minutes had gone by and the boys returned without Ruth Ann. "No sign of her," they reported.

Tensions started to rise, as well as overwhelming feelings of guilt. My heart sank as I called hotel security to give them a detailed description of Ruth and what she was wearing. As Coy and the boys went back out to search for her, I prayed that God would show me where she was. As I prayed, I was drawn to the corridor outside my hotel room. There, looking out over an atrium, I could see the floors below us. I heard in my heart, *"Call her name, loudly."* I was hesitant to yell her name, not only because I didn't see her, but also, because of what people might have thought of me if I bothered them with my yelling. Oh, the vanity! My disobedience to follow instructions caused us over an hour and a half of needless grief.

As an hour and a half had passed and still no sign of Ruth Ann, the chances of finding her seemed slim since we knew she would never wander off by herself. She knew she had to come straight back to the room. By this time, panic had set in and my search became frantic. We sent the boys to check the river area and Coy and I were to check each corridor that she would have traveled to the snack room. In between reciting the Saint Michael prayer on her behalf, and calling on Jesus' mercy, I was screaming her name, banging and kicking at every door in each corridor I went through, hoping she could hear me searching for her. Coy and I were convinced she had been abducted. The security guards gave us no good news. Every time we met back with each other throughout our search, the news was the same: no Ruth.

I was sick. My legs were weak and numb. I don't know how I remained standing. I felt like a diabetic experiencing diabetic shock. My body felt cold and clammy, my heart was racing, and my limbs were limp. I knew with all my heart my daughter was gone forever. "Someone took her, all because I was lazy and not willing to accompany her to the snack room," I kept telling myself. Rolling over and over in my mind were her words "I love you mom," and how I had taken those words for granted. There was not an ounce of hope left in my soul of finding her. At one point, I began to feel a certain sense of peace and my heart stopped racing. The realization came to me, "She must be in heaven now." It was the most sickening feeling I have ever felt, and I can hardly stomach writing about it even now.

But God granted me a reprieve. The security guards found me and told me that Ruth was safe and sound back in the room with her brothers. I was so convinced she was gone that my reply to them was, "I don't know who you found, but it can't be Ruth." The guard assured me that her brothers had confirmed it was she and that all was well. He explained that Ruth had accidentally gotten off the elevator on the floor below ours. She entered the very room below mine, thinking it was ours. The door had been propped open for maid service, and Ruth had sat there quietly eating her snack for over an hour and a half.

If I had only listened to the answer that God had so graciously granted me when I asked Him to show me where she was. I would have leaned over that railing and called Ruth's name and she would have heard me because the door was open! It wasn't until she became afraid of being alone for so long that she began to cry. The maid had noticed her crying and Ruth confided to her that she thought we had left for home without her. The maid was relieved to have found the child that she had been hearing about over the hotel security walkie-talkie system.

When I rushed up the elevator to find Ruth, the elevator indicated that it was on the third floor. As I ran to my room, however, I noticed that, just as Ruth had done, I had gotten off on the second floor. I arrived at the very room that she had mistaken for ours. Back up the elevator I went to the third floor, and there she was with her brothers. When Coy entered the room, he immediately brought us all to our knees, and we thanked God for His goodness and for His mercy on our family.

It was finally time to go to the car and all we wanted to do was get out of that place. I retrieved the car while Coy took care of last minute checkout business. When I brought the car to the loading area, I saw Coy lying on the ground with hotel staff all around him. He had held it together for so long, that with the crisis finally over, he had collapsed. Losing a child, even temporarily, is debilitating. It drains the body of all its energy stores leaving us limp.

After a few minutes, Coy regained his strength and was able to get into the car and drive us home. Not much was spoken on the long drive home—our heads were still reeling from what had just happened...or what had not happened.

The next day was July 4, and Coy woke us all up early to get us to Mass to give thanks to God for His Divine Mercy. It took months before we healed from that near catastrophe. I wasn't able to speak of it for nearly a year because of the sickness that would overcome me just thinking about it.

Later that summer, the news brought a heartbreaking story of two young eight-year-old girls who had gone missing and were never found. I mourned with the mothers of those dear girls and again got down on my knees in thankfulness for the acquittal that I had been granted.

# 17

# Early Morning Meetings

Two months before I turned forty-three I gave birth
to our fifth child, Coy John (C.J.). I knew this
would probably be my last child because of my age. I was
reminded of this fact when I had to send Coy home from
the hospital to retrieve my reading glasses so I could see
what my new baby looked like. A baby brings so much joy
to a home (especially once they start sleeping through the
night). I enjoyed watching my family grow closer through
the addition of another child. With the births of each of my
children, I recounted the words of wisdom my Aunt Laverna
once said to me, "In addition to a loving and nurturing
home, the best gift you can give to your children is siblings."
My older children learned to nurture the younger children
and I enjoyed witnessing how a new baby bends hearts. I

recall how proud my teenage son, Hudson, was when he successfully rocked our cranky new baby to sleep. Everyone had tried to sooth C.J., but it was Hudson who got to profess, "I tamed the beast!"

Being forty-three, and a new mother, I was physically tired and I felt like a grandmother instead of a mother. I repeated the age old saying, "I thought getting old would take a lot longer than this." Coy was a great delegator, as he had my older boys trained for physical duty with his routine commands of, "Boys, load the car seat for your mother." Or, "Boys, carry the baby to the car for your mother." Or, "Boys, get the baby out of the car for your mother."

Yes, youth is definitely fleeting so I began running to build up my stamina and endurance. I hated every step. Running with thirty extra pounds on my body was absolute torture, but over time, the weight came off and my daily work got a little easier. Slowly, I grew stronger and gained more energy.

About six months after C.J.'s birth, our parish priest approached me after Mass and asked me how I was doing. "Really good," I replied. He then said; "Oh, thank goodness! You were looking like death warmed over for a while!" I cried, "Father! Don't ever say that to a forty-three-year-old woman." He then said; "No, it's true. We were getting calls at the office about you." How pitiful I must have looked!

The arrival of C.J. was the perfect excuse for me to depart from my three-year venture in dance instruction. I simply no longer had any spare time to devote to dance lessons. Also, I found that even though I loved to dance, I didn't enjoy teaching as much as I thought I would. In the past, I had worked strictly with high school dance teams, and the older girls didn't require the nurturing and attention that the younger girls needed. I definitely learned that I had very little, or no patience at all, when it came to teaching other people's children. I definitely had a new-found respect for all teachers of elementary students!

It wasn't long before my days were freed up a bit enabling me to get back on the golf course. As I was playing a round of golf with three of my friends, one woman (whom I would describe as holy) told us how she rises before the rest of the household to pray. I laughed and said something witty like, "I barely rise after the household." She went on to explain that it says in the Bible we are to rise and pray before the rest of the household gets up. Still, I was not moved. Mornings were my worst time of day. If I had to be at work at 7:30 am, I didn't crawl out of bed until 7:01 am. I commended her for her diligence and then went back to focusing on beating her in that round of golf.

Since I did not take God's subtle hint the first time, God put another holy woman in my path while I was at work one day. The woman began to tell me how God recently spoke a word to her heart: "Arise." She went on to tell me that she gets up each morning to pray in silence and spend time with God. "Well, isn't this a coincidence," I said. "I was just having this same conversation a few days ago with a friend of mine. She also rises before the household to pray." I went on sarcastically explaining to her that I hope I never get that call because I hate early mornings. I simply had no extra time in the morning for prayer because I was always in a mad dash to get out the door.

Well, God is relentless when He is calling us to something more than what we are willing to accept at first glance. As I was lying in bed early one morning before I was fully awake, I followed my usual routine of asking God "What can I do for you today?" His reply: *"Get up."* Usually, He would put a word on my heart that I would contemplate all day, such as beacon, temperance, benevolence, or ardent. But this morning it was *"Get up."* Noooooo! Anything but that! I repeated my question to Him over and over again only to receive the same answer: *"Get up."*

I knew what God wanted, and for the first time I was disappointed after receiving His promptings. I did, however, complainingly, make a feeble attempt to pray.

The next morning the message was the same, and the next, and the next. It was sort of like that ground hog movie where the main character keeps living the same day over and over until he finally gets it right. I began bargaining with God for a different assignment. I then tried to pray without getting out of bed, but would only fall back to sleep. I didn't want to wake anyone else in the house by turning on the lights, so I tried going into the closet to say a quick rosary but only drifted back to sleep again.

I never needed an alarm clock. God creatively woke me up at exactly the same time each morning—5:30 am on the nose. His methods were maddening to me. My four-year-old who slept with us would call out my name at precisely 5:30 am. Sometimes the telephone would ring at 5:30 am, but I would be the only one who would hear it. Sometimes the bed would shake and wake me at 5:30 am—not one minute sooner or later. I recognized these as my morning bugle call and reluctantly, devoid of all joy, would answer Him by getting up and making a futile attempt at prayer.

After about two weeks of this constant struggle between

me and my Creator, one morning God sent my son, Hudson, into our room to speak to Coy. I didn't need to look at the clock because I knew what time it was: 5:30 am. I had already planned that if God woke me up early that day, I would just have to explain to Him why I couldn't get up to pray. Just as I had begun to explain to God why I was not going to be able to spend time with Him that morning, I felt a hand on my shoulder. I said, "What is it Hudson?" Coy answered, "Hudson's not in here. You must be dreaming." "No, I'm not dreaming," I replied, as I batted around in the dark to find who was touching me. Coy said, "Hudson went back into his room. There is no one in here." I knew then who it was, and for the first time, I made a serious attempt to be obedient to my subpoena.

I remembered I had a daily devotional somewhere in the house that Coy had given to me months earlier but that I had never opened. As I sat at the kitchen table with the lights dimly lit, feeling a bit defeated, I asked God, "What is it that you want from me?" His answer was bold and clear, yet soft and gentle. He said, *"Leslie, every day, you ask Me to "make" you holy. How do you expect to grow in holiness if you never spend time with Me?"*

I couldn't believe what He revealed to my heart. How ingenious it was. How simple. God was only trying to answer my prayer for holiness. I wasn't allowing Him to answer prayer, because I kept missing my "divine appointments."

In the dental office, we have all sorts of cancellations and missed appointments because, well, it's the dental office. No one likes going to the dentist. Sometimes our office charges a "missed appointment fee" to those patients who habitually break their appointments. Thank God I didn't receive penalty charges for all of my missed appointments with Him! I was running from God as though being in His presence was something to be dreaded or feared.

Suddenly, I was energized by this morning call of duty, and for the first time, I sincerely opened the devotional to receive what God wanted to say to me that morning. I opened the book *Jesus Calling*, by Sarah Young, to a random page, and this is what I read, (in short):

> *"Meet me in early morning splendor... while others turn over for extra sleep... you commune with the Creator of the Universe."*[9]

A page had turned in my life. A new dawn had broken as I anxiously awaited God's 5:30 am wake up calls. He faithfully woke me up every morning and I prayed devotedly for an hour and a half until I found that 5:30 am to 7:00 am was not long enough. After a time, the cock began to crow at 5:00 am. If He wanted me up at 5:00 am, then so be it.

During our quiet time in the morning, God speaks volumes to my heart. He guides me to Scripture and He communicates to me through my daily devotional. I meditate on sitting in His lap, and resting my head on His chest, like a child in the arms of her father. I close my eyes and hug His neck and rub my face across His soft beard. He cups my face in His hands and He whispers in my ear, *"You are mine."* Then, He kisses my forehead and anoints me with His blessing. He patiently listens to me as I tell Him all of my joys and concerns, even though He knows full well my thoughts before I think them. This is a relationship with Jesus.

Keeping Jesus at an arm's length while reciting prayer, and attending Adoration out of duty to Him, is not a relationship. If only I had known what I was missing all my life.

It wasn't long after our daily morning meetings began that I came across a page in my devotional that encouraged me to cling to God because trials were to come my way, and when they came, to continue trusting Him. I didn't like what I read, because up until then, everything I had read in the devotional had met me just where I was each particular day and I knew this message wasn't arbitrary.

Our savings were dwindling down to nearly nothing because of the high cost of Catholic school tuition. Over the course of twenty years, Coy had remained relatively neutral on the issue of Catholic school because he knew how much it meant to me. But He wasn't going to remain silent any longer. He had reached his breaking point when he calculated the dollar amount that we had put toward Catholic education. My explanation that we were investing in our children's salvation didn't work anymore. He was irate over the fact that he was forty-six years old, and after twenty years of hard work there was "nothing" to show for it in the bank.

I still owed ten thousand dollars in current school tuition costs, and it was again time to register for the next school year. I began to pray to God for a financial boost. I prayed fervently for over six months. Every day I begged and pleaded. I invoked all the saints and angels in heaven to pray earnestly with me, since they are before the face of God and are rejoicing over Him constantly. I went to Jesus' Mother, Mary, because I know no one loves her more than her Son. I know that He denies His Mother nothing because her will is completely infused with His. She is the ultimate disciple of her Son.

After a few months of intense prayer for my children's education, I came across a Saint Philomena prayer card. Not knowing much about this saint, I stashed the card away in a drawer thinking it was one of my children's bookmarks from school. Over the next couple of weeks, the prayer card kept popping up in strange places before me. I repeatedly stashed it away out of sight. The appearances of the prayer card continued until I succumbed to my curiosity and began reading about her.

Saint Philomena was thirteen years old at the time of her death, a virgin, and martyred. She suffered many cruel and outrageous attempts on her life because of her vow of chastity to our Lord. She was subjected to imprisonment and spent over thirty days in chains in a dark, damp dungeon. When she still refused to violate her vow that she had made to our Lord, Jesus, she was then scourged in the same cruel manner that Jesus was scourged at the pillar, in order to humiliate her even more. Her remarkable strength and miraculous healings from all of the torture she had endured only infuriated her adversaries even more. When she would not relent in her loyalty to the Lord, she was then bound and dragged through the streets behind a chariot. Even this did not bring about her death, so she was then pelted with flaming arrows, but the arrows turned back on her adversaries, killing them instead. She finally died from a lance to the neck. She endured all of this because of her love and devotion to our Lord, Jesus.

Saint Philomena became the only person recognized as a saint solely on the basis of her powerful intercessions and soon earned the title "Powerful with God." She has been known to intercede for God's help with financial problems, family problems, conceiving a baby, conversion, and many more life issues. So, I was drawn to ask Saint Philomena to intercede for me.

For those who have a hard time understanding the relationship we, who are still pilgrims on earth, have with body of the Communion of Saints in heaven, the best way I can describe the Catholic view of saintly intercessory prayer is this: I know that God is pleased with His saints and He is glorified through their adoration and their prayers to Him. No being knows the power of prayer more than those souls closest to Him. If our earthly prayer is powerful because God Himself says so, how much more influential then are the prayers of the faithful who have gone before us and are in His company?

I expect many Christians "speak" or pray to their loved ones whom they believe to be in heaven and rely on those souls to look after them. How much more potent would it be then, to rely on the prayerful intercession of the multitude of saints and angels in heaven along with the intercession of our loved ones?

Every good Christian, both Catholic and Protestant alike, prays to the saints in heaven in some form or fashion. Some people may not realize that every time we speak a word under our breath to our loved ones who have died (knowing in our hearts that they hear us) we are, in fact, "praying" (or speaking) to the saints in heaven.

There is no power in heaven or on earth greater than God, therefore, I do not expect my mother, who is in heaven with Jesus, to bypass His will and grant me my desires. That would be lunacy. I do, however, expect her, because of her love for me, to constantly place my needs before our Lord, like she would naturally do if she were still here on earth. God doesn't need prayer, but He delights in it. With the reassurance that the saints in heaven are constantly interceding on my behalf, I prayed to God for help and asked Him to take into consideration the prayers that sweet Philomena offered to Him. Daily, I asked Philomena to pray with me in my request for help with the financial matter.

I knew God understood my plight in striving to keep my children in a Christ-centered school and was pleased with my determination. I was well aware that there was no way I could feed my children the enormous amount of Truth that comes with their Catholic faith after a full day's work or in between sports, homework, and household duties. Maybe I could scratch the surface, but how many times have my children come home from school only to enhance my understanding of the faith by sharing what they learned that day?

The opportunity for my children to be afforded a Catholic school education was crucial to me, because I know that it is only through knowledge of our faith that we are able to recognize the mendacity that has engulfed our secular culture. Money in the bank did not concern me. I was willing to spend it all and do whatever I could to keep my children steeped in their faith, but it concerned Coy, and therein laid the problem.

For nearly forty days I prayed a novena to this young saint, asking for her assistance in my prayers to God. I asked her to pray with me as I begged for the Divine Mercy that I know Jesus readily offers. Divine Mercy chaplets accompanied all of my other morning prayers and contemplations. I was faithful and I knew God wanted to grant me the desire of my heart because my desire for Catholic education was good.

I know that when our desires are for the greater good and we have faith in God's ability to turn any situation into an opportunity to receive His bountiful blessings, we can and will receive all that we ask…and more.

One morning as I sat in prayer, I realized there was no hope in the near future of receiving the answer to my prayer for the money I needed to keep my children in Catholic school, so I surrendered completely, waving the white flag. I had no more prayer left in me. I felt like I had run a race but came in dead last. I repeated over and over to God that I surrendered completely to Him and that I accepted the path He was taking me on, even if it was His solemn will that my children were to lose their gift of being able to enjoy a Catholic education. I asked God to change my heart so that I would be able to accept His will.

As I had my eyes closed in prayer, I saw an image of a young, skinny girl with dark, long hair. She was staring at me, solemnly. It lasted for only a fraction of a second and I wondered what I had just experienced. Could that have been dear Philomena? I knew that God allowed visions of His saints at particular times in order to soothe us and reveal His messages to us. I recalled how Cooper was allowed to see visions of my mother, not through her own power, but by God's power and goodness. God is gratified in His saints and enjoys letting them serve Him through their intercessory prayer for us.

When I arrived at work that morning, I unexpectedly found at my workplace an envelope with my name on it, written in Dr. Schilling's handwriting. Inside the envelope, I found a check for ten thousand dollars. I couldn't believe it! I was so humbled and thankful that God saw fit to hear my prayer. I knew then, the vision I had earlier that morning was Saint Philomena coming to reassure me that my prayers had been heard.

I went to Dr. Schilling and thanked her and I asked her why she gave me so much money. She answered, "You've been a loyal employee for so long and I wanted to give this to you as a thank you for all of your hard work." When I asked her what I was supposed to do with it, she replied, "Whatever you want."

God used Dr. Schilling to bless me that day, as He has used her many times before. She had no idea of my dilemma, but because she is such a faithful woman, she responded to His tugging on her heart with enormous generosity and no questions asked.

That evening while I was contemplating the day, Hudson came to me and said (not knowing the events of the day), "When you were praying this morning, God woke me up and told me to go pray with you, but I was too tired and when I wouldn't get out of bed God said to me, *Hudson, is it that hard?*" and I told Him, "Yes, it's too hard." I could sense the feelings of guilt that were weighing on Hudson, and I knew that the next time God called him to prayer, he would be obedient.

While visiting with the Lord the next morning, I set a Bible aside for Hudson just in case God called on him again. At 5:45 am, Hudson staggered into the living room. He had received his orders and he was obedient. I then proceeded to explain to Hudson the miracle of the day before and why

God desired his prayer on that particular day. He prayed for about thirty minutes with me and couldn't stay awake any longer, so back to bed he went. I understood fully how he felt, and I was proud of his effort to respond obediently to God. I knew over time he would grow stronger and more diligent in His response to God's call for him, but early morning rises were my call of duty, not his...yet.

# 18

# My Idol

There is a constant metamorphosis of our hearts and souls that eventually, if we choose, brings us to completion in Christ. Our purpose on earth is to love. God is love; therefore, when we love perfectly, we are perfect in Christ. When I was a child, I was full of love for God and others. It felt good and natural to love. Why then, as an adult, can it be so hard to love sometimes? Maybe, it is because love is a *choice*. Maybe, it is because it's hard to see others as Christ sees them. Christ tells me to forget about myself and focus on Him and others. It is hard to place others before myself when I am accustomed to being self-centered. I have to make a conscious decision to put myself in third place—God first, others second, with myself third. Even if I do this with cursing under my breath, I know eventually the habit will become comfortable and my heart will slowly be affected by the change in my behavior.

It's like running. My heart didn't get stronger the first day. It took weeks before my heart benefited from the exercise and eventually running got easier. It actually felt good. What is true about repetitive sin is also true about repetitively making good choices: eventually it becomes natural.

One morning as I was rolling out of bed for my morning meeting, I started repeating the words "Saint Ignatius. Saint Ignatius." I knew God was sending me a message, yet, I found no real evidence of what He wanted me to know about Saint Ignatius in my morning prayer, so I simply invoked Saint Ignatius to pray for me that I would find what God was leading me to.

Later that day as I was sitting in my bedroom, lo and behold, a book that had been tucked tightly among others on a high shelf (at least six inches from the edge) came crashing down, making quite a commotion. It was the old devotional that I had studied with my prayer group years before. It landed open, face down, and I couldn't wait to grab my reading glasses to see what message God had waiting for me.

As I opened the book, my eyes went straight to the top of the page to which the book was opened, and there it was, the following quotation taken from *The Spiritual Exercises of Saint Ignatius*. It read:

> *In every good choice, in so far as it depends upon us, the direction of our intention should be simple; I must look only to the end for which I am created, that is, for the praise of God our Lord and for the salvation of my soul. Therefore, whatever I choose must have its purpose to help me to this end.*[10]

I immediately went online to order the book, *The Spiritual Exercises of Saint Ignatius*, and couldn't wait to begin reading it. Once it arrived, I spent a large portion of my time with the Lord working through the intense exercises. Initially, I reviewed sin and its effects on creation from the sin of Lucifer to the original sin committed by Adam and Eve.

Then, the hard part came when I asked God to show me my sins. We spent three days "discussing" my sins for nearly the entire two hours of our morning meetings. God's spirit showed me how I stab Him in the heart every time I willingly choose to sin.

Each morning I was sickened to the point of tears by what God was revealing to me about myself. I felt like God was purging me of all my ugliness—not what I see in the mirror in the morning, but the ugliness in my soul. He showed me my obsessiveness toward outward beauty, material things, and my impatience with others. We discussed my desire to be first, best, and well esteemed.

Taking a good hard look at myself was frightening. I wished I could unzip my body and remove the wretched hag that coils herself up inside of me like some creature out of a sci-fi movie. I have asked God many times for the remedy to remove her, and His prescription for a hag-free soul is GRATITUDE. A grateful heart melts away pride, envy, hate, selfishness, and all common ailments of the soul.

In the diary of Saint Faustina, she writes the words of Jesus as spoken to her;

> *"A soul's greatest wretchedness does not enkindle Me with wrath; but rather, My heart is moved toward it with great mercy."*[11]

After three days of taking a good hard look into my cold heart, I was completely drained of all joy. It was only then that I was finally ready to move on to the next exercise. God wanted me to understand myself on a deeper level and Saint Ignatius' book was definitely the tool I needed to help me do just that.

Each day is a learning process. I can read all the books written about conversion of heart, but applying what I read is the hard part. Despite the spiritual growth that God is leading me in, I continually fall back into my weakness for material things, vanity, and basically, SELF—except now it is usually accompanied by guilt. In this case, guilt is good. It is a sign of progress. Slow progress is at least progress.

On my birthday, I was delighted to come across some absolutely adorable shorts that I convinced myself I had to have. I was so proud of how good I looked in them that I bought four pairs of them! I just knew this was God's way of wishing me a happy birthday, especially since they were on sale! "It was meant to be!" I thought.

Do you see how the mind can play tricks on us? I definitely was not discerning who was doing the talking in my head at that moment, because truthfully, I didn't want to hear anyone else's voice but mine.

Well, I paid for my poor choice for three days afterward. God wasn't going to let me slip back into my old routine especially after all of the hard work we had recently gone through.

Each morning as I sat in prayer, I was unable to focus. Those shorts kept popping into my mind, accompanied by a tiny bit of guilt. I immediately put the thought out of my mind and tried to focus on the Lord, but nothing came, absolutely nothing. My sin of obsession over material things, even as simple as clothing, had blocked me from hearing God that morning. Deep down, I didn't want to admit that it was my choices that separated me from Him.

Day two came, and the same scenario unfolded. I tried to avoid what was pulling at my heart yet I was unable to connect with God. On the third day, after an hour of "forced prayer," I finally put my book aside and said, with these exact words, "Okay God, let's talk about those shorts." His calm and Father-like voice spoke softly to my heart, *"What's the problem with the shorts, Leslie?"* He made *me* tell *Him* what the problem was. He wanted me to admit that all along I knew I was putting material things before Him and that my obsessive behavior was damaging.

"Please, please, don't make me take back those shorts. I love those shorts!" I pleaded. Then He made my heart stick in my throat when He replied, *"More than you love Me?"* "Yes, I guess I do love them more than I love you," was my pitiful answer to Him! Doesn't that sound ridiculous? It was! How embarrassing!

Obviously, I loved those shorts more than I loved Him, because I was willing to be separated from Him because of them. Now who's the idiot?

Once I had decided I would take back all four pairs of shorts, I was free and I was able to sit in prayer again. God then spoke to me again saying: *"Now, open your book and let's do our meditation."* So, I opened my book, *The Spiritual Exercises of Saint Ignatius*, and the subject was the first commandment.

---

*"You shall love the Lord your God with all your heart, with all your soul, with all your mind, and with all your strength."*

*Mark 12:30*

---

I was led to contemplate the things that I loved more than the Lord. Well, that was easy. I just "fessed" up to it not two minutes before. Oh, how good God is, showing me how I made material things my idol.

I had to cure myself of my weakness of wanting material things. I thought to myself, "Can I go one year without buying anything for myself?" I dismissed that thought immediately saying, "Now, that's just crazy talk." A second time, out of the blue one day during ordinary chores, the thought came to my mind again, "Can you go one year without buying anything for yourself?" "Ha, that's crazy," I retorted, and again I dismissed the thought. While I was cleaning my patient's teeth, the thought came again for a third time, "Can you go one year without buying anything for yourself?" My response was, "Yes, Lord, if I do it for You."

I vowed then I would not purchase any clothing, shoes, purses, or anything of that nature for myself for one year. I had tried this before during Lent, but forty days just isn't long enough; there is a light at the end of the tunnel. Anyone can stand on their head for forty days, but a year…maybe that was just what I needed to break free of my obsessive habit. I had asked God to show me my sins, and He did, and it was up to me to let Him guide me in overcoming those sins.

God will always give us a way out, because He does not want us bound by our bad habits that keep us from Him. If we truly want to be reconciled with God, we have to be willing to look at ourselves from the inside out and have the courage to accept God's plan of action to rid us of our "disorders."

———

*"Do not store up for yourselves treasures on earth, where moth and decay destroys, and thieves break in and steal. But store up treasures in heaven, where neither moth nor decay destroys nor thieves break in and steal. For where your treasure is, there also will your heart be."*

*Matthew 6:19-21*

———

# Part Three

# Conversion

# 19

# Humility

I know my obsession with materialism was holding me back from reaching the next level of maturity that God had designed for me, but really, no lesson has been harder to learn than my lessons in humility. My ego was so inflated that God let me jump right out of my three-inch heels into a pigsty of pride, and as I wallowed with the swine, I found a pearl. It was humility.

Constantly, God has to remind me who I am and who He is. As I was preparing to lector at Mass one day, I forgot that I was merely a messenger in the service of the Mass and began to focus more on my appearance as if I were about to be in the spotlight of center stage.

This particular day, I dressed in my favorite cream-colored pants and smart matching top. My hair was pulled back just right so that my beautiful, fake-gold, dangled earrings would show off nicely. And of course, to top it off, was the perfect pair of three-inch, matching, cream-colored heels.

The church was particularly full that day. Sacred Heart Catholic Church is a magnificent, semi-Gothic structure that can hold over eight hundred people easily. When it was time for me to read the Scripture, I made it all the way to the podium (ambo, but few people know it is called that), when I realized I did not have my reading glasses with me. I froze in fear and whispered to Father, "I forgot my glasses!" He nodded, allowing me to go back to my seat and retrieve my glasses. As I was proceeding back up to the ambo, I was sure all eyes were on me, and you can bet they were—they were trying to figure out what I was doing.

Well, God granted me just what I had longed for all my life, the attention of everyone in the room.

Just as I was reaching the steps, I thought to myself, "I'm late," so I decided to hurry up a bit. Then it happened. Down I went. My foot came out of those fabulous heels, and as I hit the ground I grunted, "Ugh!" Nearly in unison, the whole congregation responded, "UUGH!!" Father jumped up and came rushing over to me, asking whether I was all right, and all I could say was, "Humility."

I clip-clopped, one shoe on and one shoe off the rest of the way to the ambo. My hair had fallen out of its holder and my bra strap was down my arm. I was a mess. As I turned on the microphone to read, I had an urge to say something witty but thankfully, God pinched my lips shut and said to me, "It's not about you." It was as if I answered back, "Yes, sir," and I read the Scripture like a professional. I never missed a beat. When I was finished, I turned to Father and said once again, "Humility." He just smiled and said, "You recovered well."

I then clip-clopped back to my shoe that I had left on the step and picked it up, leaving my pride where my shoe had fallen, and I returned to my seat. I got just what I had wanted that day, attention. God got just what He wanted: MY attention...again. I'm sure God said to Himself, "Mission accomplished...for now."

Two weeks later I was scheduled to lector again and this time I was a little more cautious in my wardrobe planning. I kept it simple, yet classy, and still a little shell shocked from coming out of those three-inch heels the time before, put on some nice shoes with lower heels. Also, to ensure I would in no way forget my reading glasses again, I devised a plan to keep them at the ambo. Before mass, I slid my glasses into a cubicle to the right side of the ambo where the lectionary would be placed after the reading. I was convinced all was well until it was my turn to read. When I went to retrieve my glasses, I mistakenly looked on the left side of the ambo, not remembering I had placed them on the right side. They were GONE! "Oh no, not again," I thought.

I frantically searched for my glasses while seconds ticked off the clock and the parishioners looked on anxiously, waiting for me to begin. Finally, I looked on the other side of the ambo and found them tucked right where I had put them. I was extremely humiliated and upset about the fact that I couldn't remember where I had put my glasses not fifteen minutes before. This time, I did not recover well. I tried to speak but my tongue was three-feet thick. I stumbled my way through the Scripture like an infant learning to walk on a downhill slope. It wasn't pretty, and if I'd had my druthers, I would have preferred falling down again.

The whole thing that got me into this mess was the fact that I had forgotten why I wanted to lector at Mass. Before lectoring at any Mass, I had always said a prayer asking God to speak through me and to make me invisible; not allowing me to be a distraction so the listeners would look past me and only hear His word. As I had grown accustomed to reading at Mass, I had forgotten to pray that simple prayer.

After my two humiliating experiences, my next attempt to read the Scripture at Mass was successful. As I prepared to lector once again, I didn't avoid my three-inch high heeled shoes. I put them on and marched boldly into Mass confident that this attempt would be successful because I had finally figured out my problem. As I knelt in prayer, I asked God for His forgiveness of my sins, and I asked that He make me invisible this time so that no one would notice me, but only hear the words of the Scriptures that I was to read. I asked the Holy Spirit to flow through me and into the hearts of the parishioners that day.

Everything went well. My heels held me up, my reading glasses were in hand, and my confidence was in the right place—in God.

The next morning at the dental office, my patient popped up saying, "Leslie, I just feel compelled to tell you something. When you were reading at Mass yesterday, all I could think of was how beautiful you were and that you looked like a model." I thanked her and laughed at the irony of it all…when I desire to be invisible and ask the Holy Spirit to flow through me, then, and only then, am I most radiant.

I realized it wasn't my high heels that made me topple

over that humiliating day, and it wasn't forgetfulness that made me fumble in the ambo for my glasses the next week. It was my pride. Both of those catastrophes were the result of my making the ministry of proclaiming Scripture all about me. Once I came to my senses and remembered that I was merely a messenger, I was able to read with true sincerity of heart.

*"...for everyone who exalts himself will be humbled, and the one who humbles himself will be exalted."*
*Luke 18:14*

I have to admit that I have a talent for reading and telling a good story. I also have a strange attraction to microphones! I am convinced that God gifted me with these talents and "attractions" and in turn, I truly want to glorify Him through them. But I got a little sidetracked. I started thinking about myself and lost focus a bit. God knows my sincere heart. He knows I want to do something, anything for Him. Sometimes He just has to rein me in a bit and remind me Whom I am serving and that my service is not about me.

It's easy to make our service to God about us. Nobody loves praise and compliments more than me, so I speak from many years of experience when I say it is easy to fall into the trap of dedicating our time and hard work in service to God just so that we can be noticed and commended for it.

When I was helping with a major project for our parish, I met up with a woman who works tirelessly for the community. Everyone knows her and is astonished by her good and diligent work. But one day while working alongside her, after about an hour I grew weary of listening to her boast of all the good deeds she has done for the community. Blah! Blah! Blah!

*"Take care not to perform righteous deeds in order that people may see them; otherwise you will have no recompense from your heavenly Father."*
Matthew 6:1

The sad fact is this woman didn't need to say a word, because we had already witnessed her generous giving for years. Most importantly, it didn't matter whether we knew about her service, because the One who would reward her for her work had already seen it and recorded it.

It is when I am in the presence of people like this woman that I am reminded to be humble in my actions and know it is only God that I should care about pleasing. We all love to receive praise and compliments for our good works, but we need to bear in mind that humility goes a long way in the company of others.

Like that generously hard-working woman, I want to make a difference! I know God is God, but surely he needs my help, right? Needs it? No. Desires it? Yes. I want to keep busy with His work because I know it pleases Him while it satisfies my restless heart. God delights in our zeal to serve Him, I am sure of it. After all, it is God Himself who places within us the longings of our hearts to serve Him.

We will never know the magnitude of the impact that

our encouragement and stewardship have on those we serve. When we speak the Truth, it has the power to travel distances beyond our imagination. It travels from one mouth to the next, one text to the next. Years ago, there was a commercial for a hair shampoo with the slogan "and she told two friends, and she told two friends, and so on, and so on, and so on." Don't be afraid to tell the Truth. It just might travel to the ends of the world and save a life.

I have the privilege of sponsoring a young twelve-year-old girl named Maria, who lives in the Philippines with her brothers, sister, and parents. I chose her picture from several others of children who were in need of financial assistance. I support her financially each month. I correspond regularly by letter with this sweet young girl and we encourage each other to keep with Christ. Her picture remains on my refrigerator to remind me and my children that our service to God can reach around the world and doesn't need to be locked up inside the boundaries of Muenster, Texas.

---

*"Before I formed you in the womb I knew you.*
*Before you were born I dedicated you… To whomever*
*I send you, you shall go; whatever I command you,*
*you shall speak."*
*Jeremiah 1:5,7*

---

I am blessed through her letters telling about her life in the Philippines and showing how a simple life with very little material wealth can be the happiest life. America is distracted by all sorts of things, but Maria reminds me of what is most valuable: time well spent working and praying and enjoying family and friends. Her mind isn't occupied with a video game all day or worrying about what she is to wear. She lives a humble life, with her attention focused on what truly matters: family and service to God.

We are invited to have a personal relationship with Christ, but to stockpile His goodness for ourselves is not what He wants. He wants us to share our blessings with others. We are here for only a short time, and there is so much to be done! Serve! Service to God through serving one another is the best exercise we can do for our heart.

God wants us to spread His messages of hope and love to the world and calls each one of us to some sort of work for the greater good. He wants us to be obedient to His promptings no matter how we "feel." Seek out what God requests of you. He will gladly let you know, by the desires of your heart, what He wishes for you to do for Him. Relax, He won't ask you to do anything outside of the perfect personality and talents that He has equipped you with.

Everyone has something to give—everyone. By giving, we receive abundant blessings in return. Take a leap of faith! Do something, anything, just DO something! But remember, we are not called to "do" in order to earn, rather, we are called to "do" out of pure and simple love for God.

I think about my young son C.J. who loves to "help" with washing the dishes, and how he makes a bigger mess of things than if I would have just done it myself. I allow him to "help" because I know he wants to please me and he feels a sense of pride in doing something good for his mother. The same must be true for God, even when I mess up all sorts of things I recognize that He is pleased with my desire to serve Him and that He is perfectly content with making lemonade from my lemons.

As we advance in our faith, God increases His requirements of us. He isn't content with letting us stay in one place in our faith journey. He is continually giving us tasks that challenge us to trust and exercise our faith more fully. Our service to God should grow more intense with each spiritual growth spurt. As in learning to read music, we must first learn the scale, but eventually God expects us to play something beautiful.

———————

*"What good is it, my brothers, if someone says he has faith, but does not have works? Can that faith save him? If a brother or sister has nothing to wear and has no food for the day and one of you says to them, "Go in peace, keep warm and eat well," but you do not give them the necessities of the body, what good is it? So also, faith in itself, if it does not have works, is dead. ...Do you want proof, you ignoramus, that faith without works is useless? Was not Abraham our father justified by works when he offered his son Isaac upon the altar? You see that faith was active along with his works, and faith was completed by the works."*

*James 2:14-17, 20-22*

———————

# 20

# The Cellist

When I turned forty-five, I realized half of my life was probably over and I started to reassess some of my life goals. I wanted to travel and go places—like Branson. I was going to attend the symphony and take Ruth Ann to plays and the ballet. Most of all, I was going to learn to play the cello! For nearly ten years I had yearned to play the cello. It is one of the most beautiful instruments I have ever heard. The students at the Christmas program made it look exciting, and if a young girl could learn to play it, so could I.

I thought the cello sounded best when two played in harmony, so I decided that Ruth should take cello lessons with me. She had three years of piano experience, but the cello was something foreign. We didn't know what we were getting into, but we looked forward to lessons. We contacted the music department at the local university and were provided a list of all the available instructors for a wide array of instruments.

I chose the most American name on the list under cello instruction: Eugene. I emailed him inquiring about lessons, but he didn't respond to my request. "Okay, now who?" I thought. Next, I chose Lejing. Lejing promptly replied to my email and agreed to give us lessons.

I purchased two cellos off the internet and set our practice time. We were off and running! So we thought. I had never learned to read music, nor had I ever played a musical instrument before. I did, however, study music theory as a dance major in college, but it applied primarily to movement and not to reading the music. So, I knew it was going to be a long uphill battle, but I really had no idea of the grand scale of it all. (That was a great pun if you caught it.)

I was eager to begin the first lesson while Ruth was only willing to go along with the whole idea because she was excited about going out to dinner and shopping afterward. Rarely would we travel into the city without including one of those two treats.

As we climbed the steps to Lejing's apartment and tapped on the door, we were a little nervous about stepping out of our comfort zone into something new. The door opened and there he was, Lejing. When I saw him, there was a tiny ping in my heart, like a homing device. Although I couldn't put my finger on it, I knew there was something special about him. I had this same type of feeling only twice before in my life when meeting a stranger: the first time, when I met Coy, and the second, when I met my brother's future wife, Danielle.

Danielle was a nurse at my obstetrician's office when I was pregnant with Ruth. Each time she opened the door to the waiting room to greet me, she appeared as if she were glowing. I was drawn to her but didn't know what was so special about her. Never-the-less, with each visit, the moment I saw Danielle, it was like angels singing. For nearly eight months I couldn't figure it out. Then, just before my six-week follow-up visit after Ruth's birth, it dawned on me: "Jason is supposed to meet her!" My youngest brother, Jason, was in his mid-twenties and had not yet found that perfect woman to marry.

I couldn't wait to tell Jason about her. It just happened that Jason was scheduled for a dental cleaning only a few days after my revelation. As he was sitting in my dental chair, I said to him "Jason, I met your future wife." Well, as you can imagine, there was a long silence, followed by a sigh. His reply was "Oh, Leslie…" I didn't relent. I told him that Danielle was the one, and how I had known it from the beginning, but didn't know it. I urged him to go by the office and meet her, but he knew that would be extremely awkward. So, to appease his sister, he settled for letting me talk to her first, and if she agreed to give him her phone number, he would then pursue it.

My appointment with my obstetrician was just a few days away. I knew it would be my final appointment with him because he would be releasing me from his care. That meant it would be my last opportunity to see Danielle, so I had to make my case for Jason a good one. I rummaged through my photo drawer like a maniac, trying to find the best picture I could of Jason, and I couldn't wait to tell her about him.

As I entered the examination room that day I was teeming with excitement because I had finally figured out Danielle's radiant glow. I ranted like a crazy person, as she will testify, and explained that she should meet my brother. She retreated hastily and told me she wasn't interested in a relationship, and quite frankly, wasn't sure if she ever wanted to get married. "Nonsense," I said, "You just haven't met the right person yet!" I convinced her to let me give her cell number to Jason, and she reluctantly did so. I could hardly wait to call my brother. I told him the good news that she was willing to meet him, and he kept his part of the bargain by asking her out on a date. I will make this long love story short: Jason and Danielle did meet that weekend on a blind date, fell instantly in love, and married. They now have three children.

Just as I had with Coy and Danielle, standing in Lejing's apartment, I again had the feeling that I was meeting someone special. I knew that somehow this twenty-seven-year-old Chinese man and I were supposed to meet, but I wasn't sure why. I did know, however, that it would have very little to do with cello lessons.

In my 5:00 am meetings, I had inklings to pray for this young man that I had just met so I offered Lejing to our Lady, the mother of God, asking her to protect and guide him. I assumed he wasn't Christian, because I noticed tacked on his wall, a list of thirty commandments. I couldn't read what they were at the time but I wondered what religion had thirty commandments. I have a hard time obeying the Ten Commandments, how can anyone follow thirty?

At our next lesson, I made it a point to ask Lejing what religion had thirty commandments, my finger pointing to the yellow sheet of paper tacked to the wall. Looking stunned at first, he then realized I was talking about a sheet of paper that he and his roommate had as a reminder about the "thirty commandments" of cello...something or other.

Week after week I was drawn to Lejing's peacefulness, tranquil demeanor, and gentleness. His very loving, soothing, and reassuring nature was Christ-like, but I knew in my heart he did not yet know Christ.

Through Lejing, I witnessed patience and humility like I had never seen before. God has placed many people in my life to teach me many things, but patience, gentleness, and humility was something new. I knew God was continuing His lessons in humility with me, but I hoped this time it wouldn't be as harsh as falling on my face in front of eight hundred people. Actually, falling on my face in front of Lejing each week was worse.

Cello lessons were brutal. That instrument was a real beast. Or maybe I was the beast, but one of us needed to be tamed! The one-hour lessons were devoted to monotonous practicing of the scales, proper finger placement on the strings, reading the music, and intonation. But if someone asked me what I learned in cello, my answer would be "humility." Humility was taught in two different forms. The first was by observance—Lejing was the model of humility. The second form was more painful and violent; it was the act of perseverance in "taming the beast." The beast really wasn't the cello after all; it was my pride. But "The Beast" remains to be the name I have given my poor innocent cello because after all, it reminds me of the taming that is yet to be.

I am used to being good at the things I do. If I am not

good at something, well, I just don't do it. I am a good golfer, a good dancer, a good dental hygienist, a good wife, and a good mother. It's hard to do something you're bad at when you're full of pride. Each lesson I felt like Lejing chiseled off a little bit of my pride. Week after week I went home defeated yet determined all the more to prove to myself, and to anyone else who cared, that I could play the cello. We struggled for a full year learning scales and intonation and short pieces of easy music. I loved it and hated it at the same time, and Ruth just flat hated it. She traded in the cello for her piano and I eventually traded in my student cello for a "better" one.

I looked forward to my weekly lessons, and after a year of instruction under my belt I felt that I was ready to begin playing at Mass. I convinced myself that I should play at the Easter Vigil Mass accompanying the beautiful mixed choir. Two days before the Mass, while practicing with the choir, I realized I was a suckling in my cello playing and there was no way I was ready to play in front of people, especially accompanying the piano and choir. Panicking, I texted Lejing the whole scenario and asked him whether he would come play with me. He responded almost immediately. I could tell he was absolutely mortified by the thought of me playing in church in front of three hundred people or more, or playing anywhere for that matter! He agreed to come to my rescue. Whew, crisis averted.

Lejing played beautifully, of course, while most of the time I didn't know what line of the music we were on. If I did play the correct line, I'm sure it was so out of key that Lejing was forced to play even louder to cover my mistakes. My attempt at playing the cello was a fiasco at the very least.

Another hard lesson in humility was learned that night. Thank goodness Lejing was there to keep me from ruining the beautiful music of the Mass.

It wasn't until Lejing had come to play the cello with me at Mass that I understood with more clarity the tugging that I had in my heart, that "homing device" that pinged every time I was in his presence. A few nights after the Easter Vigil Mass, I was awakened with Lejing weighing heavily on my mind so I began to pray, asking God, "Why is my heart yearning for him?" God answered me so clearly that night. He said, *"Because I yearn for him and I have placed that upon your heart."*

That was it! The homing device! I realized then that Lejing was not meant to be at that Holy Mass for my sake, it was for *His* sake. What in the world made me think I was ready to play the cello at one of the most important Masses of the year? God knew I wasn't ready, but more importantly, He knew I would panic and call Lejing to help me. It wasn't about me at all; it was about Lejing!

Traditionally, the Easter Vigil Mass is only celebrated after nightfall. It is customary for the congregation to enter into a completely dark church where they are given an unlit candle. The absence of light represents the state of the world before God sent His Son, Jesus, to redeem mankind from the darkness of sin. Once the celebration begins, the only light visible is the single flame that is lit by the priest, exemplifying Jesus as the Light of the World. From that single flame, each member in the congregation awaits the illumination of their candle. The flame passes from one person to the next, thus, symbolizing Christ's Truth spreading throughout the world. Once all the candles are aflame, the lights in the church are then turned on signifying that Jesus has overcome the darkness.

As Christians, we are all called to be a beacon of light for those who have not yet come to know the Truth of Jesus Christ. As I lit Lejing's candle from mine, I could not deny my calling to bring the Light of Jesus to him. But what I found most interesting was the part of the Mass where the candles were re-lit and Lejing used his candle to inflame mine. There is definitely a dual purpose for Lejing and me. I am certain that, somehow, I am to lead him to Christ and Lejing is to lead me closer to Christ. Learning how to play the cello is just the icing on the cake!

Morning after morning, God placed Lejing at the forefront of my thoughts and would lovingly say to me, *"Bring him to Me."* My reply was always the same, "Lord, I don't know how. Show me how." It was as if God had thrown a slab of meat on a plate in front of me and said, "You're ready for solid food. No more spoon-feeding." For months my morning prayers were intense. God placed upon my heart a love so strong for Lejing that I felt like I couldn't have loved my own children any more than I loved him. I even asked God, "Why do I love him so?" God's reply was clear, *"It is necessary. If you didn't love him, you wouldn't pray for him."* I knew God was right.

I accepted my summons and prayed fervently for months. The months dragged into a year, and then another year, and another. I couldn't stop praying for him even if I tried. When I resisted praying for him, the urge to pray became more intense. Some days I prayed unceasingly. Even though I went through the motions of the day, all of my thoughts and actions were secondary to prayer for Lejing. I knew for sure this time I was heading to a mental sanitarium. I prayed that I wasn't crazy. The more "normal" I tried to be, the "crazier" I became. I fought against what I knew God was calling me to do, but the more I fought, the harder He held on.

I begged God to help Lejing find his Son, Jesus, fast, because I felt like I was going to burst from my aching heart for him. God sent a clever reply through a witty patient and friend of mine with whom I was confiding in one day. While shrugging her shoulders and applying her lipstick, she simply said, "Oh well, if you burst, you burst." She told me to go ahead and burst if I must, but to gather myself together and be diligent in pursuing patience, knowing all things come in their proper order.

Each time I prayed I asked God for His direction. I pleaded my case before Him that I was not equipped to bring a Chinese Buddhist to conversion to Christ and that I'm merely a dental hygienist. His answer was always the same.

———

*"My grace is sufficient for you."*
*2 Corinthians 12:9*

———

I reminded God that I wasn't schooled in theology at a level such as this and that I could never debate with effectiveness the Truth of Jesus. But God gently calmed my heart and revealed to me that He chose me for a reason and that I need only to love Lejing, nothing more. God led me to Saint Paul's letter to the Ephesians, where I was reminded that He provides for me and equips me with all that I need to carry out His mission.

*"I will equip you for the work of the ministry."*
*Ephesians 4:12*

I wasn't supposed to begin cello lessons ten years ago when I first had the inkling. I wasn't supposed to take lessons from Eugene. I was supposed to meet Lejing. The lessons I am to learn from him greatly exceed the cello. He is to bring about in me a conversion of heart. He is to draw forth from me the patience, endurance, and humility that God desires of me, and I am to draw him forth to Christ through those very virtues that he already owns. He has so many of the attributes that Jesus possesses, yet, he lacks Jesus.

Several mornings during prayer for Lejing, a popular Christian book came to mind and I dismissed the thought until a patient of mine arbitrarily commented on that very book. I thought about the book briefly and how I had ruminated over it earlier that day while in prayer for Lejing. Well, by now, I had learned God's cadence, and when the third patient mentioned the book, I knew I was meant to buy it and give it to Lejing.

A little nervous in this adventure, I found a book by the same author that had a similar tone to the one I had been thinking of. So, I purchased it instead. While reading the book, I was pleased by what the author had to say, until near the end, when he made a statement that I disagreed with. I became frustrated with the author and vowed I was not going to give that book to Lejing or any other book by that particular author for that matter!

I put the whole book idea aside and forgot about it until a few months later when I was shopping on the internet for school clothes for my children. Two different times already that day, I had gone online and purchased school pants for my sons. I put my items in my cart and emptied the cart each time. It was what occurred the third time I was making an online purchase that day that got my attention. I had gone back online to buy little boy's shoes for C.J. When I found the shoes, I asked Coy to check to see whether they were the ones we needed to get C.J. for his school uniform. Coy confirmed the shoes were the right ones and he added them to the cart.

When I went to check out, I noticed my cart had two items in it. I questioned Coy about what else he had put in the cart. "Just shoes," he said. When I opened my cart I found the two items: size eleven little boys' shoes and "the Christian book" that God had originally placed on my heart to give to Lejing. Starring in disbelief for a few moments, I asked Coy whether he had put the book in the cart. "No, just shoes" he replied again.

I realized that God didn't change His mind about giving that book to Lejing. I was the one who had changed course, but God always finds a way to get me back on track with HIS will, not mine. "Thy will be done." I purchased the shoes and the book and vowed to God that I would deliver it, even though I didn't want to. I worried that Lejing would think I was some sort of religious fanatic. Even if it were so, I didn't want to display it so openly. My obsessive worry about how others perceive me unfortunately dictates my behavior, unless I know I am being given a direct order from God. Then I dare not disobey.

When it came time for my next lesson, I climbed the steps to Lejing's apartment with great difficulty. My legs were weak. I felt as though they were going to buckle beneath me. Why was I so worried about giving this book to him? Well, basically the answer is pride and vanity. I didn't want him to think I was crazy for giving him a book about Christianity, knowing he was Buddhist.

I placed the book nonchalantly on Lejing's desk and never mentioned it until it was time to leave, when he tried to give it back to me, thinking I had forgotten it. I didn't know what to say about the book and I certainly wasn't going to say "God wants me to give this to you," so I pushed it back into his hands and said, "It's for you to read later." He smiled and took the book back into his apartment. I felt like I had just dodged a bullet.

I knew God was pleased with my obedience, but I was a little disappointed with myself in how reluctant I had been to carry out such a simple task that I knew, without a doubt, He wanted me to do. I felt like a coward. How can I say, "I trust you Lord," then buckle when He gives me a simple assignment? I felt like I was "all talk and no action." Why was it so hard for me to hand a simple book to the gentlest person on the planet? Again, all I can say to that is…what a rookie.

I know that God has placed Lejing in my life for a special purpose. It is not for me to see the divine plan that God has orchestrated. I am only to be His faithful servant and follow His lead. I pray for Lejing every day and sometimes I grow weary of it. I worry about how, when, what if…I ache with constant concern for him. I can't bear the thought of Lejing going through life not knowing Jesus' infinite love for him. I grow impatient not seeing the fruit of my labor. I ask, "When, Lord, will I see the fruit of my prayers?" His answer was and is always the same: *"It is not for you to see. You would not be able to handle it. You need only have faith and trust in Me."* I begged for some sign, anything to let me know that I wasn't just going crazy. One morning before work, I asked God for a sweet message of reassurance that I was on the right track and that He was indeed hearing my prayers. Because I asked with faith, He delivered.

That morning was particularly busy at work. While I was seeing my full load of scheduled patients, Dr. Fuhrmann (Dr. Schilling's lovely niece who had joined the dental practice) asked me to come into the next room and evaluate her patient for periodontal disease. I was reluctant to examine her patient because my schedule was already tight with my own patients. I knew it would take too much of my time and my schedule was already running behind. I went through the steps required to examine the patient for disease and informed her of her periodontal condition in the least possible amount of words and quickly exited the room to get back to my own patient. But then I remembered that I had not given her the required informational packet for patients with periodontal disease, so I gathered my literature and re-entered the room.

After I gave my spiel to the patient and delivered the literature to her, she began to tell me a story. I listened halfheartedly while my mind was elsewhere. She sensed my inattentiveness and then said something loud and clear. She boldly professed, "God puts people from opposite ends of the world together for a reason."

I stopped in my tracks and immediately thought of Lejing. Now she had my full attention. I said to her, "I agree with that." Just then, she did the craziest thing. She jerked as if she just remembered something that she had forgotten, and said, "Oh! I have a message for you." Then she did something very bizarre…she began to cry. She walked over to me and touched my shoulder and said, "You're on target…and don't worry about that boy anymore, God has a special place set aside for him in heaven." I didn't know what to say. I was speechless. That was one of the few times in my life I was absolutely speechless, devoid of all commentary. I simply smiled at her and left the room. I went back into my dental operatory and cried with relief. I thanked God for displaying His great love for me by having sent such a powerful message in a most unexpected and impressive manner.

Embarrassed by my rude exit, I decided to go back and thank the patient for her kind words. When I thanked her, she said to me, "God uses me to deliver messages… and He uses you too, you know." Again, I stared at her dumbstruck.

That "periodontal patient" never returned to our office, and I knew in my heart she wouldn't. She had served her purpose that day. There was no need for her to come back. I know with all my heart that my prayers for dear Lejing have been heard and God's divine plan is unfolding in his life.

With Lejing's thirtieth birthday approaching, I struggled for weeks over what sort of gift I was to give him. I wasted so much time and energy trying to think of the perfect material gift. While praying for direction, God revealed to me that the gift I was to give to Lejing was Him. I was to tell Lejing about Jesus' love for him. What a perfect gift.

As I sat in prayer, contemplating the wonderful works that God must have done to prepare Lejing's heart for Jesus, a soft voice whispered in my ear, *"Leslie, it wasn't Lejing's heart we were preparing. It was yours."* My answer to God was, "Of course; it had to be." Alas, another lesson in humility.

For Lejing's present, I gathered my thoughts and wrote them down in a five-by-seven card, on the cover of which was a painting of Jesus, entitled, "Prince of Peace," by the eight-year-old artist, Akiane Kramarik, who had visions of Jesus while she slept. Miraculously, she was able to paint in great detail the face of Jesus, depicting Him exactly as He appeared in her dreams. Inside the card, I wrote everything I felt compelled to explain. I wasn't nervous this time. I was just the messenger that day. I felt like I had graduated from rookie status to veteran.

The following morning in my meeting with Jesus, I was like a little girl awaiting praise from her father for doing something good. I thanked God for the long journey of prayer that He had placed me on for Lejing, and I was ready to kick off my shoes and relax, thinking it was all over, until God said to me, *"Leslie, you were like a wild horse growing weary trying to get out of the starting gate. Now the gate is open and you're running…and the journey has just begun."*

Sometimes I run ahead of God and want results quickly and easily. But good things are worth waiting for. Sometimes I have to close my eyes in the morning and picture myself asking Jesus whether I can stand on His feet so that I can stay in tempo with Him. He lets me stand on His feet, and then we dance. He is content with keeping my feet on His, because He knows that I must let Him set the pace and not get out of time, because patient endurance obtains everything…

*"Lord, guide my steps in ways of grace that they may ever be in harmony with the music to which You have set this world."*[12]

This was the prayer on the plaque that my mother bought for me in that gift store so long ago. It is remarkable how it applies to every chapter of this book…and every chapter of my life.

I know God would not have set Lejing and me on this course just to have us go in circles. I continue to pray with thanksgiving for my answered prayers for Lejing, even though my eyes do not yet see the evidence of my answered prayers. I am confident that Lejing will successfully bring me closer to Christ through our perseverance in "taming the beast," and through my privilege of knowing someone so Christ-like—him.

Hopefully, one day I will be able to write about the great adventure that God has put Lejing and me on, but for now, I must let go of my grip that I have on Lejing and trust that he is in the safest place he can be: God's hands, not mine.

# 21

# Conclusion

At a company lunch one day Dr. Schilling instructed us to place our orders for lunch. My order included a chocolate pie. Not just a slice, but a whole pie. When our lunch was delivered, my coworkers were excited to see a whole chocolate pie arrive. They chuckled to themselves about the fact that I was brazen enough to request a whole pie. My response to them was simple: "You won't get pie if you don't ask!"

The same is true with God; we need only ask with faith, knowing we will receive it. Throughout my life, I have found there is no limit to what God will do for me through His Son, Jesus. He delights in my complete dependence on Him for everything and showers me with grace and favor... simply because I ask.

I'll never forget a clever quote that my dear aunt Carol said to me one day as a reply to my overzealous confidence. She said, "Girl, you're not conceited, YOU'RE CONVINCED!" She was right! I was, and still am, convinced that...

*"I can do all things through Him who strengthens me."*

*Philippians 4:13*

God Himself had planted seeds of faith in my heart that I would find a fairytale husband, and He brought those seeds to maturity. When I was a child He placed within me a genuine love for others and the desire to serve. He has developed that desire in my adulthood by giving me a servant's heart. He blessed me with the conviction that right is right and wrong is wrong, even when the world tells me differently.

God continually guides me on the path that He has set before me, gifting me with the assistance of His angels and the many different people I have encountered along the way. We are not put on this earth to make the journey alone. We are always given divine assistance. The people in our lives help steer us on or off course. They are all part of our own personal route guidance system. My GPS has been my parents and grandparents, siblings, husband, my children, Dr. Schilling, the faithful in the community, Gretchen, the crazy old man down the lane, the butcher, the caramel candy gift giver, the periodontal patient and all of my patients through whom God has spoken, holy women, a six-year-old boy, the Catholic priest, the cellist, Mary the mother of God, the Communion of Saints, and His many angels in disguise.

As I mentioned in the foreword, I do not know where I am going, and sometimes the narrow gate is hard to see through the fog of sin, but I believe in what I hope for and I am certain of what I do not see. This is my faith. This could be your faith.

Faith is God's free gift to us because of His infinite love for us. If we were able to earn His love and all of His blessings, there would be no need to be thankful for anything. When we earn something because of our actions that "something" is owed to us and rightfully ours, but when we are given a free gift we are inclined to be grateful.

A grateful heart opens the floodgates to God's blessings, overflowing and piled up. The world today tells us we "deserve" good things (even to the point of excess), as if somehow good things are owed to us. No one deserves anything. As a matter of fact, I do not want what I deserve, because I dread the loss of heaven and the pains of hell as a result of what my sinful self deserves. It is only through God's love and mercy that we are blessed with so many good gifts.

Some people have gifts heaped up and surrounding them but haven't opened them yet. Accept the gift that Christ has given you: eternal life in heaven. Don't leave it sitting right in front of you unwrapped. Accept God's will for your life, NO MATTER WHAT, and your life will be overflowing with good treasure and happiness. He will pour His rich blessings and good favor upon you in unbelievable ways.

Ask God to mold you into the person He desires you to be. We are all made from the mold of Christ's image; however, we need an adjustment every so often. Sometimes it is necessary to take a good look at ourselves to see what we've become, or where we're going.

The next time you look into the mirror and see the hag (or beauty queen) that has taken up residence, look past the surface. Look deeper into the soul and evaluate what needs improvement and what needs to be whittled away. It's hard to whittle on ourselves, but when we let the Master Carpenter refine us and redefine our edges, we become Christ-like from the inside out.

This is beauty we can't buy in a bottle at the department store. No face lift, tuck job, or expensive cream can make us truly beautiful. After all, our surface beauty only lasts until we open our mouths, then it is our true character, the inner beauty (or haggishness), that is reflected in our words and actions.

———————

*"...for from the fullness of the heart the mouth speaks."*
*Luke 6:45*

———————

Never give up striving for inner beauty. Keep gratitude stocked up in your medicine cabinet and take a healthy dose daily. When you feel like you don't need it anymore, take two doses! Keep faith in your hearts, knowing without a doubt, everything that is good, right, just, and perfect can be achieved through the One who loves us. Just believe, and stop guessing and questioning and worrying. It's like my ordering a whole pie: you just need to ask with faith, believing that you will receive what you ask for.

If I ever question the power of faith and what can be accomplished through it, I need only read Hebrews, Chapter 11. It is a great summary of the remarkable things that were accomplished through ordinary people who had extraordinary faith in God:

"*Faith is the realization of what is hoped for
and the evidence of things not seen.*"
*Heb. 11:1*

"*By faith we understand the universe was
ordered by the word of God.*"
*Heb. 11:3*

"*By faith Abel offered to God a sacrifice
greater than Cain's.*"
*Heb. 11:4*

"*By faith Enoch was taken up so that he
should not see death.*"
*Heb. 11:5*

"*By faith Noah, warned about what was not
yet seen, with reverence built an ark for the
salvation of his household.*"
*Heb.11:7*

"*By faith Abraham obeyed when he was called to
go out to a place to receive as an inheritance; he
went out, not knowing where he was to go. By faith
he sojourned in the promised land.*"
*Heb. 11:8-9*

"*By faith he (Abraham) received power to generate
even though he was past normal age—and
Sarah herself was sterile.*"
*Heb. 11:11*

_____

*"By faith Abraham, when put to*
*the test, offered up Isaac."*
*Heb. 11:17*

*"By faith regarding all things…Isaac*
*blessed Jacob and Esau."*
*Heb. 11:20*

*"By faith Jacob, when dying, blessed each*
*one of the sons of Joseph."*
*Heb. 11:21*

*"By faith Joseph, near the end of his life, spoke*
*of the exodus of the Israelites."*
*Heb. 11:22*

*"By faith Moses was hidden by his parents*
*for three months after his birth."*
*Heb. 11:23*

*"By faith Moses, when he had grown up, refused*
*to be known as the Pharaoh's daughter; he chose*
*to be ill-treated along with the people of God*
*rather than enjoy the fleeting pleasure of sin."*
*Heb. 11:24-25*

*"By faith he left Egypt." Heb. 11:27*

*"By faith he kept the Passover and sprinkled*
*the blood, that the destroyer of the first born*
*might not touch them."*
*Heb.11:28*

_____

---

*"By faith they crossed the Red Sea as if
it were dry land."
Heb. 11:29*

*"By faith the walls of Jericho fell." Heb. 11:30*

*"By faith Raheb the harlot did not
perish with the disobedient."
Heb. 11:31*

---

The many verses listed are just part of one chapter in the Letter to the Hebrews. We have a whole Bible filled with examples of persons who were granted divine favor beyond reason. They were able to accomplish great things and unfathomable feats through their faith in God!

My all-time favorite example of faith in the Bible is found in the Gospel of Mark. It is the story of a woman who suffered from a hemorrhage for twelve years. She was so filled with faith that she knew with all her mind, heart, and soul all she had to do was touch the hem of Jesus' garment and she would be healed. When she touched His hem, it was her faith that released Jesus' healing power. Jesus felt the power go out from His body and He turned to ask, *"Who touched me?"* When He saw the woman, He said to her;

*"Woman, your faith has healed you." Mark 5:34*

I want to be that woman! She was able to release healing power from Jesus as if it were as easy as turning on a switch. I want to have that kind faith! I want my children to KNOW that kind of faith so their lives will be filled with God's goodness and favor and JOY no matter what their circumstances. We all have the gift of faith through our baptism. It is a seed that is planted in our hearts. It is tangible. We all have the ability to tap into it and receive the tools necessary for abundant living.

Faith is a mindset that "all is well" because our loving Father is all good and no matter what happens in this world, we are secure. It takes patience and daily prayer to truly understand what simple faith can bring to us on a daily basis and on a grand eternal scale. We shouldn't settle for trudging through the day, looking forward to happiness after this life in heaven. No, God wants more for us. It is faith nurtured on a daily basis that makes our lives here on earth rich and fulfilled.

I urge you; spend time with the Lord, the giver of our faith. Read the manual on how to remain faithful, the Bible. Don't go it alone. The directions are in black and white easy to read print and best of all, there is no gray. It's okay to get worn out. God will rejuvenate us. Hang on and don't ever stop running the race! Ponder the resolve of Winston Churchill when he said, "Never give in. Never give in. Never, never, never, give in."

I presume he meant never "give up." So, I dare to encourage you to always give in. Always give in. Always, always, always give in to the Lord by surrendering to His Holy Will for your life. Then you will have the courage to "never give up." Keep plowing forward to the prize: heaven. Trust that God doesn't lie, and most importantly, take consolation in the fact that anything can happen when we *Factor in Faith.*

―――

*"For we walk by faith, not by sight."*
*2 Corinthians 5:7*

―――

# Epilogue

The "author's apology" in the epilogue of the Second Book of Maccabees, sums up my thoughts quite well, so I shall steal his words and let him speak for me as I bring "*The Faith Factor*" to a close.

*"I will bring my story to an end here. If it is well written and to the point, that is what I wanted; if it is poorly done and mediocre, that is the best I could do. Just as it is harmful to drink wine alone or water alone, whereas mixing wine with water makes a more pleasant drink that increases delight, so a skillfully composed story delights the ears of those who read the work. Let this, then, be the end."*

*2 Maccabees 15:38-39*

# References

1. The New Catholic Answer Bible, (Wichita KS: Fireside Publishing, 2011)

2. Francis Cardinal George, foreword to Handbook for Today's Catholic, Revised Edition, (Barnhart, MO: Liguori Publications, 2004)

3. Charles L. Allen, God's Psychiatry, (Old Tappan, NJ: Fleming H. Revell Company, 1953)

4. Johnette Benkovic, Women of Grace, (San Francisco, CA: Ignatius Press, 2016)

5. Charles L. Allen, God's Psychiatry, (Old Tappan, NJ: Fleming H. Revell Company, 1953)

6. Redemptrist Pastoral Publication, Handbook for Today's Catholic: Revised Edition, (Barnhart, MO: Liguori Publications, 2004)

7. Saint Joseph Catholic Radio, prayer card "Eucharistic Miracle of Lanciano, Italy," (Orange, CA: Saint Joseph Catholic Radio)

8. Charles L. Allen, God's Psychiatry, (Old Tappan, NJ: Fleming H. Revell Company, 1953)

9. Sarah Young, Jesus Calling, (Nashville, TN: Nelson, Thomas, a registered trademark of Harper Collins Christian Publishing, Inc., 2004)

10. Saint Ignatius of Loyola, The Spiritual Exercises of Saint Ignatius, translated by Anthony Mottola, Ph.D. (New York, NY: Doubleday, a division of Bantam Doubleday Dell Publishing Group, Inc. 1964)

11. Marian Fathers of the Immaculate Conception of the B.V.M., Diary of St. Maria Faustina Kowalska: Divine Mercy in My Soul © 1987 Excerpted from Divine Mercy Minutes with Jesus: Praying Daily on Jesus' Words from the Diary of St. Faustina by Rev. George W. Kosicki, CSB (Stockbridge MA: Marian Press, 2010)

12. Author unknown, this was the prayer printed on a plaque my mother purchased for me as a teenager.

Ruthie Hess (Mom)

Frankie Hess (Dad)

Leslie age 5

Fairytale Husband Coy

Gregg, '85-86

Jason, '85-86

Leslie at Texas Stadium, 88-89

Nursing Home visit with DCC, Leslie Ezelle, man unknown, Leslie Hess, '88-89

DCC Show Group "waiting to perform" Leslie with Carista Ragan and Nan Stutts '88-89

Leslie and Coy

Back Row L: Tanner, Cooper, Hudson; Front Row L: Ruth, Coy, Leslie, C.J.

Danielle and Jason Hess

Leslie and Sondra

Gretchen and Leslie

The Butcher

Dad

Nephew Strider

Dad

Jason, Dad, Leslie, Gregg Hess

Dr. Elaine Schilling

John Louis and John

The Cellist

Grandma Hess, Aunt Laverna, Aunt Mary